DESIGN: PAPER

© 2012 Rockport Publishers

First published in the United States of America in 2012 by
Rockport Publishers, a member of
Quayside Publishing Group
100 Cummings Center
Suite 406-L
Beverly, Massachusetts 01915-6101
Telephone: (978) 282-9590
Fax: (978) 283-2742
www.rockpub.com
Visit RockPaperInk.com to share your opinions, creations, and passion for
design.

10 9 8 7 6 5 4 3 2 1

ISBN: 978-1-59253-771-6

Digital edition published in 2012
eISBN: 978-1-61058-390-9

Library of Congress Cataloging-in-Publication Data available

Design: Public School

Printed in China

DESIGN: PAPER

A Seductive Collection of Alluring Paper Graphics

Public School | Austin

Rockport Publishers
100 Cummings Center, Suite 406L
Beverly, MA 01915

rockpub.com • rockpaperink.com

CONTENTS

INTRODUC-TION

Cody Haltom
Public School
Austin, Texas

I'm not breaking new ground by telling you that a shift is happening—has happened—in visual communication's primary medium, from ink and paper to pixel. Designers on the younger side, myself included, are constantly hearing that they may be working primarily in digital design if they want to survive. This is very likely true, but paper's role in graphic design is certainly still alive, even if it is losing its grip as the popular choice.

Companies still need business cards (for now). Products still need packaging. Who wants to send out an invitation for that special day via email?

This transition from print to digital is affecting the designer in a number of ways. Some, of course, are negative, but one positive is this: It's making us more appreciative of the chances we get to work with paper. What was once a given is no longer, and these opportunities are all the more exciting because of this.

The majority* of pieces in this book, regardless of category, share a consistent aspect: paper selection is an integral part of the project. Paper is no afterthought here. Icons weren't slapped on to the cheapest white stock that could be found. This work was enhanced by the paper choice, not burdened by it, and a change in paper choice would drastically change much of it.

The categories in this book represent most of the traditional areas paper has a hand in, and a relatively fresh face known as papercraft, which is expanding paper's role in the design process. Once used as a platform to hold a message, paper is now being used as the message.

I am happy to say that much of the work in this book comes from designers who fall on the younger side of the design world. Sure, there are some familiar big hitters, but many are working their way up, and doing so with printed work in a digital age.

The essays throughout the book were written by designers who regularly inspire me with a strong appreciation and understanding of paper and its many qualities. I would like to thank them for taking time to give insight into their process and paper's role in it.

Finally, I would like to thank everyone who submitted work to this book. This has been a great learning experience for someone who definitely has more to learn on this subject.

A few were chosen because they look great and they use paper.

IDENTITY

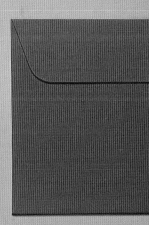

WASTED OR SACRED?

Jett Butler
Föda Studio
Austin, Texas

2,200 years of spreading ideas—poetic or pragmatic, dangerous or trivial, mundane or revelatory—rendered in a simple combination of ink and chlorophyll.

Until now. Now, paper is anachronistic, slow, and cumbersome. Becoming environmentally conscious, we've learned the true value of the tree and the pulp. Paper is potentially irresponsible, clumsy, taking up space.

Digital proliferation is undeniable. Pixels and ones and zeroes are necessary. The ability to bypass a letter carrier in order to communicate via IM, text, or email makes paper seem akin to a smoke signal.

This revolution is somewhat perfect: Let pizza coupons, airline tickets, product manuals, bills, quick notes, lazily written magazines, and poorly composed photos move to the cloud. Paper is too important a resource—too expensive, too materially consumptive, too slow—to be taken for granted or treated carelessly with that bullshit.

We'll save the fiber for those things that we cherish.
We'll keep the pulp for what matters.
We'll press it carefully now.
We'll keep it in shoeboxes under the bed, in frames on the wall, in our wallets and purses. We'll wrap it around vinyl records, hide it in safes, and place it under our windshield wipers. We'll pass it from one hand to another when we want to make a communiqué more humane.
We'll use it to sketch out our ideas.
We'll clutch it to our chest.
We'll blot tears.
We'll crumple it.
We'll burn it in protest.
We'll nail it to the door.
We will recycle and start anew.

Eight Hour Day USA

Mikey Burton   USA

ian@duomatic.ca | 1 403 802 0350
Let's share some ideas.

DUO   Canada

Judith Augustin Germany

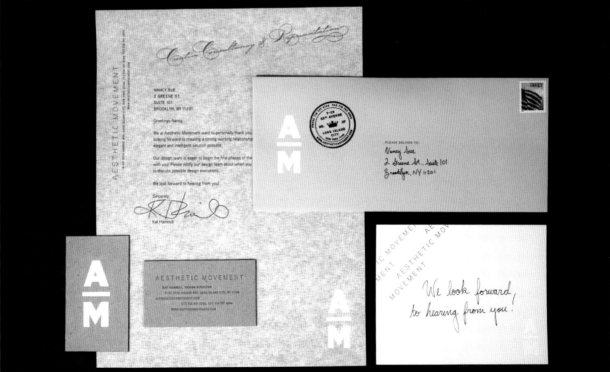

Aesthetic Movement   USA

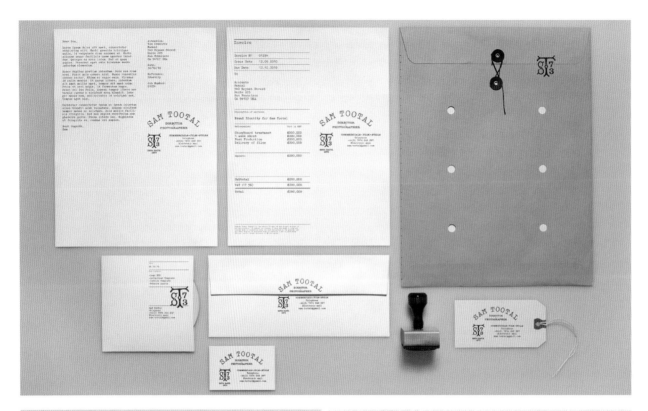

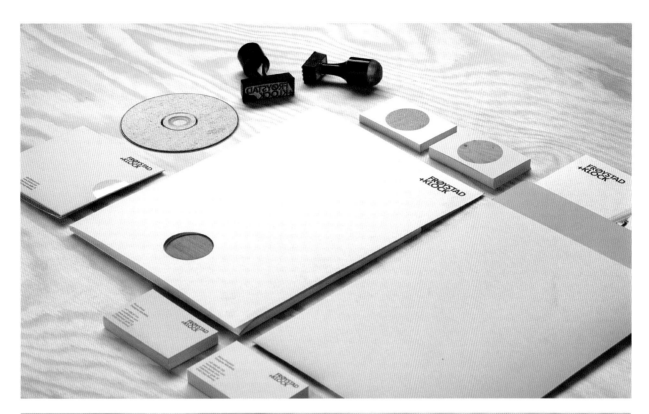

Heydays Norway

CLOSER LOOK

The Consult

England

Identity for a written communications firm called Bang Your Own Drum, a long-time collaborator of The Consult.

Drumstick pencils add an additional playful element.

A single piece of yellow stock enhances the upbeat nature of the identity.

BANG
YOUR
OWN
DRUM

The focal point of the business card is
succinctly captured on a drum skin.

BBDO Designworks   USA

Foreign Policy   Singapore

Brown & White Creative   England

Mash   Australia

Brandcentral   Ireland

Mikey Burton   USA

CLOSER LOOK

Foreign Policy
Singapore

Shanghai's first gastro-bar that serves up tapas-style modern European cuisine. It is set in a sleek and simplistic interior that encourages social interaction by sharing portions over a long communal table.

The business card, which folds into a table, is designed in reference to the long communal tables used in the restaurant.

Kraft and newsprint paper, used throughout the identity, are representative of the simple, unpretentious environment. The metal clips further add to the rustic look.

Utilizing stamps with inexpensive resources like kraft and newsprint help create a brand that is easy to replicate and falls in line with the experience of the building.

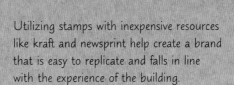

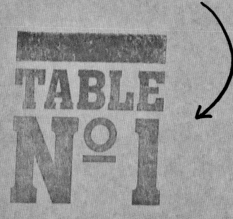

by Jason Atherton

Brigada Creativa Spain

Agoodid   Sweden

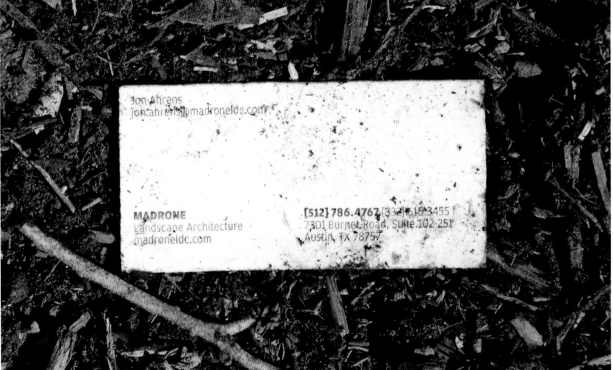

Föda Studio   USA

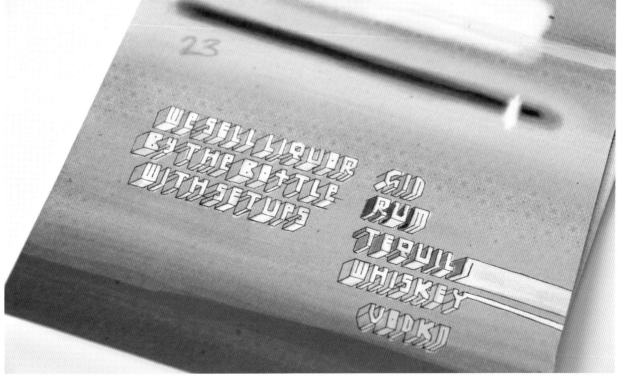

Föda Studio   USA

Foreign Policy   Singapore

Fuzzco   USA

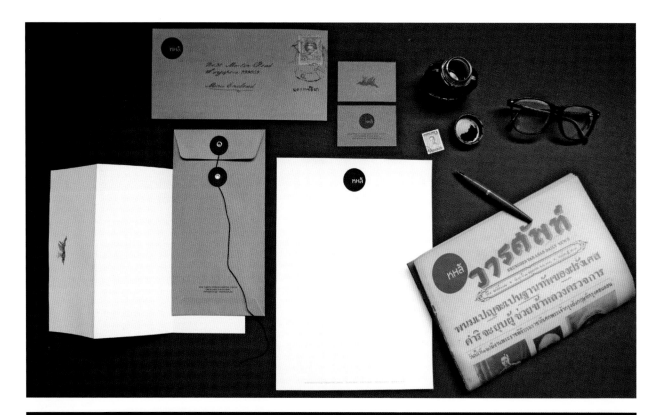

Foreign Policy   Singapore

Foreign Policy Singapore

CLOSER LOOK

Lundgren + Lindqvist

Sweden

Identity for Johanna Lenander, a writer and editor, living and working in New York City.

Bold colors used throughout add a modern twist to an identity based on the editorial traditions found in classic newspapers.

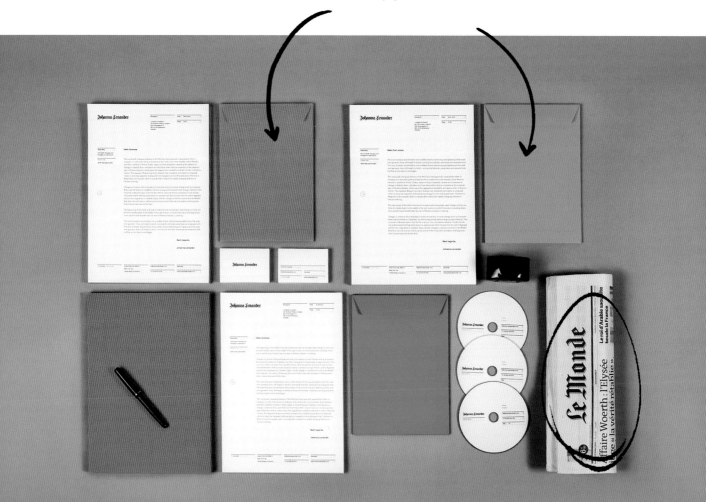

A small dose of color from
the back of each piece acts
as a nice accent on the
other side.

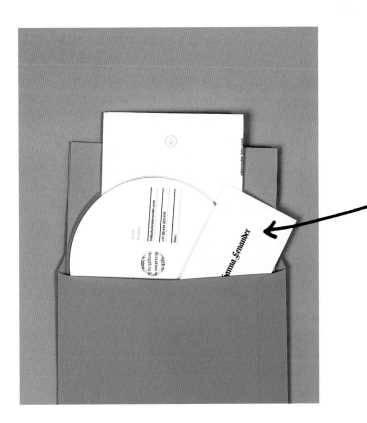

High-quality stocks paired with crisp
design elements work to create an
identity that feels very thoughtful and
craft oriented.

Hatch Design   USA

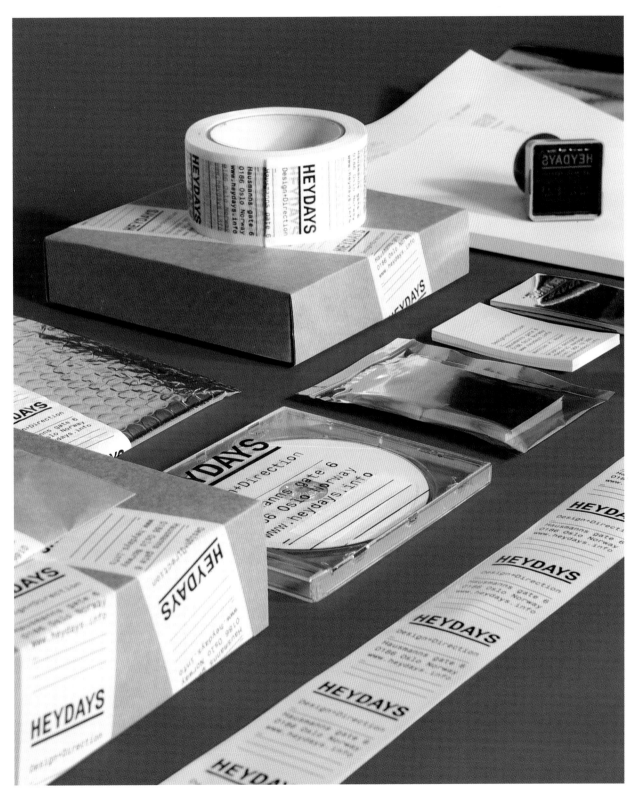

Heydays Norway

Heydays Norway

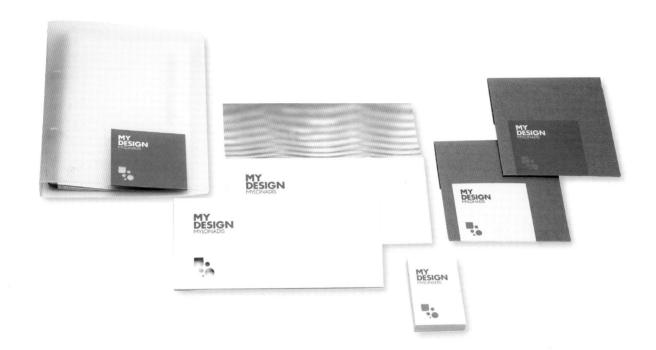

Kanella   Greece

Blok Canada

Blok   Canada

CLOSER LOOK

Bond Creative Agency
Finland

Identity for Pino, an interior decoration shop
in Finland

The name, which is Finnish for "pile" or
"stack," is cleverly represented in the *I*
of the logotype.

The colorful identity works well against the neutral palette of the store's interior.

The multitude of colors in the identity also references the stacks of colorful items on the shelves of the store.

James Prunean   Canada

Kanella   Greece

Mami Awamura   USA

Mami Awamura USA

CLOSER LOOK

RoAndCo Studio
USA

Ten Over Six is a fashion boutique named after the price tag for 10/6 (10 pounds, 6 pence) on the Mad Hatter's hat.

Inspiration was taken from the vernacular of contemporary price tags.

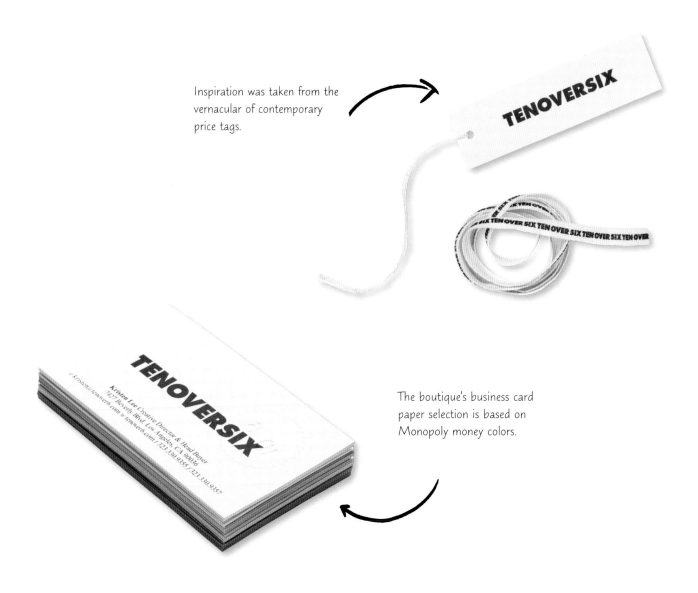

The boutique's business card paper selection is based on Monopoly money colors.

Gold "discount" stickers are used throughout the identity.
It works as the brand's signature shape.

Root   England

Mark Pernice   USA

Matt Chase USA

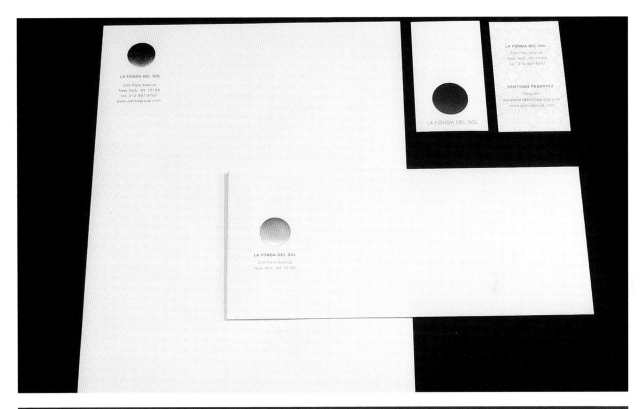

Mirko Ilić   USA

Poff & Freimuth Unlimited   USA

Poff & Freimuth Unlimited   USA

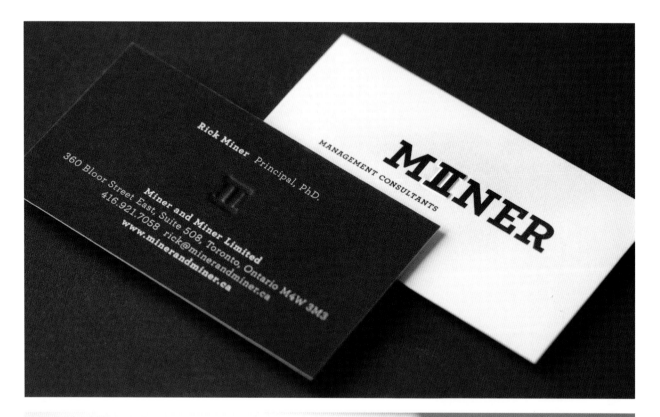

Matter Strategic Design   USA

Javas Lehn Studio USA

CLOSER LOOK

Watson and Company
USA

Launched in 2009 by Daniella Luxembourg and Amaila Dayan, Luxembourg & Dayan is a private gallery located in the Upper East Side of Manhattan.

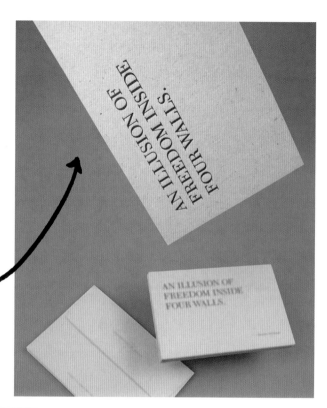

The chipboard is a nice contrast to the refined materials.

A single color helps the identity stand out from an otherwise traditional black-and-white gallery color palette.

Simple, thoughtful paper choices are combined with beautifully set type to create an elegant identity.

LUXEMBOURG & DAYAN

64 EAST 77TH STREET NEW YORK NY 10@

75 · P 212 452 4646 F 212 452 4656

LUXEMBOURG & DAYAN

64 EAST 77TH STREET NEW YORK NY 10075

LUXEMBOURG & DAYAN

AMALIA DAYAN

Because Studio　　　　　USA

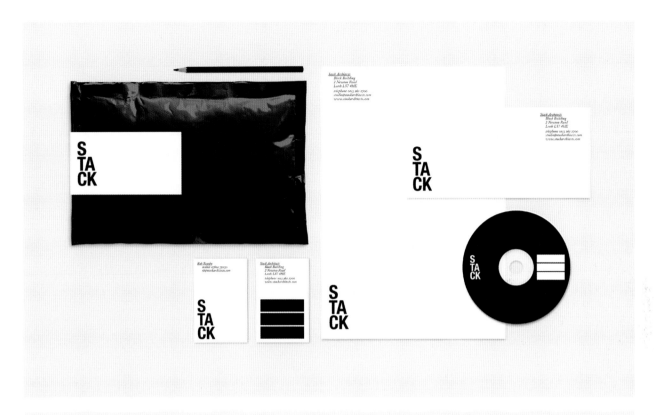

The Consult   USA

The Consult   England

Hello Tenfold USA

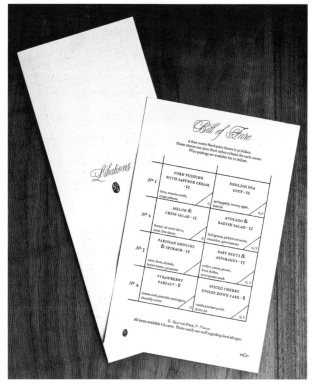

OMFGCo.   USA

Fabio Ongarato Design   Australia

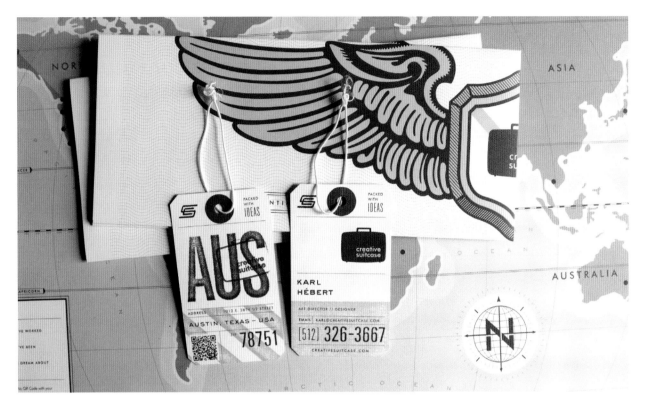

Creative Suitcase   USA

CLOSER LOOK

Föda Studio
USA

The identity for Michael Hsu, one of the
pre-eminent modernist architects in Austin, Texas.

Beautifully considered typography and
thoughtful paper selection help reinforce a
minimal feel to the identity.

Michael Hsu
Office Of Architecture

3423 Guadalupe Street
Suite 200
Austin, Texas 78705

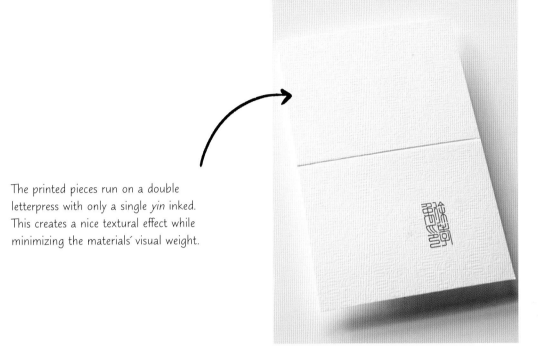

The printed pieces run on a double letterpress with only a single *yin* inked. This creates a nice textural effect while minimizing the materials' visual weight.

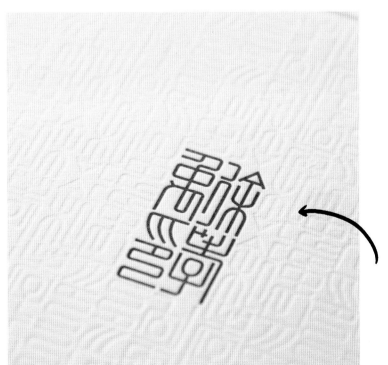

The family's seal (or yin) was up-dated in a redrawn logogram.

anne elizabeth
writer
Ae@thepracticedaccident.com
thepracticedaccident.com

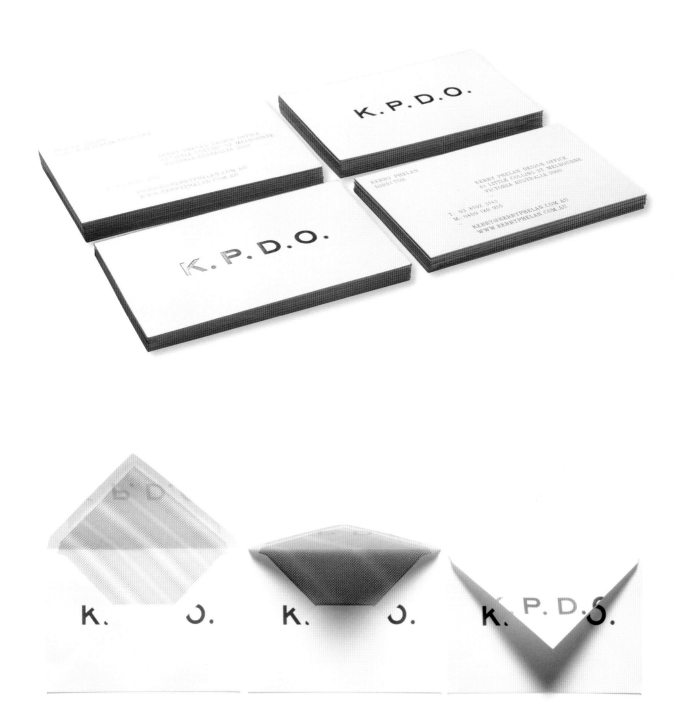

Fabio Ongarato Design USA

Foundry Communications USA

Stitch Design Co.   USA

Thumbcrumble   England

Root   England

CLOSER LOOK

Departement
Canada

Personal identity for Departement,
a multidisciplinary creative studio.

The identity relies on a number of stocks, adding
texture and color without being heavy handed
with design elements.

Small envelopes house the studio's business cards and give a quick introduction.

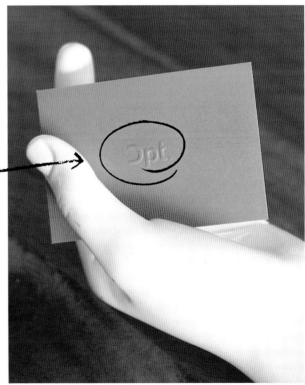

Printing is subtle throughout the identity, acting as texture and letting the materials shine through. The subtle nature plays well against some of the bright colors used.

Departement   Canada

Matchstic   USA

Brogen Averill New Zealand

Brogen Averill   New Zealand

CLOSER LOOK

Because Studio
England

Low Winter Sun is a consultancy specializing in developing innovative, creative, cooperative, and environmental projects.

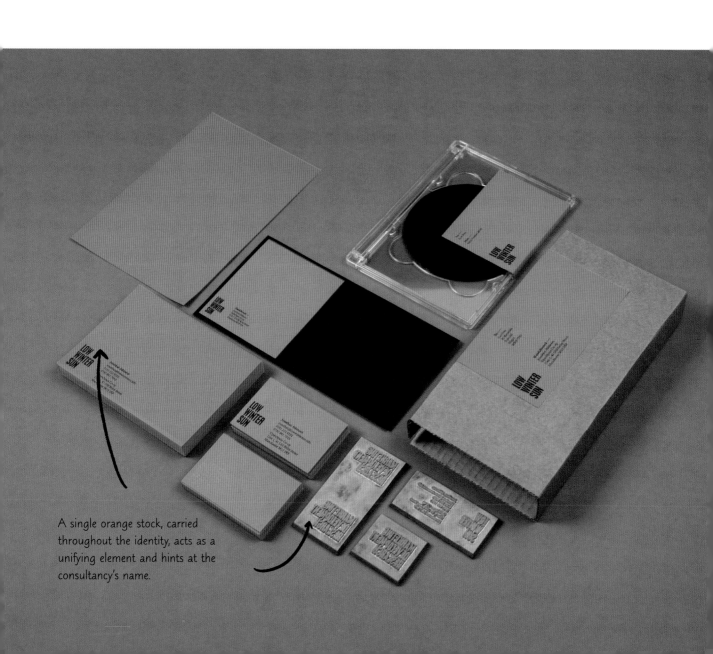

A single orange stock, carried throughout the identity, acts as a unifying element and hints at the consultancy's name.

Low Winter Sun's services are arranged in the same way as the logotype on the back of the business cards.

The bold logotype, located in the same place on all material, also plays on the name and, when paired with a single color, creates a stark feel.

Brogen Averill   New Zealand

A Friend of Mine   Australia

Beacuse Studio England

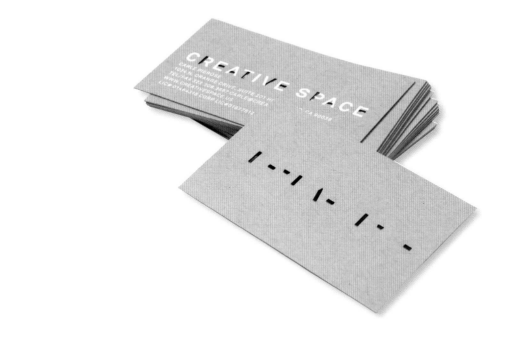

RoAndCo Studio USA

Blok   Canada

Real Estate Arts   USA

PURVEYORS OF

Product Superior

LIMITED

FINELY CRAFTED GOODS

GET IN TOUCH

with

PRODUCT SUPERIOR

nifer Blanco and John E

+

INFO@PRODUCTSUPERI

47) 743 7621 **FAX** (347

W.PRODUCTSUPERI

PER GOODS ar

PRINT

NICE TO SEE YOU AGAIN, READER.

FOR OUR SECOND ANNUAL PUBLICATION WE'VE CHOSEN A **SUPERB** SELECTION OF TALENT, IF WE DO SAY SO OURSELVES, (WHICH WE DO) **PLEASE ENJOY** AND IF YOU HAVE ANY ISSUES WITH THE ISSUE, TALK TO **KYLE**

FOREWORD BY EDENARD   PRINTED IN IL   DESIGNED IN BROOKLYN & CHICAGO   PIES

Our Contributors

Fogelson-Lubliner, Timothy Goodman, Rob Morris, The Free Associates,
Ben Pieratt, Zissou, Scott Reinard, Colin Matriel, David Iglesias,
Foster, Jones Stone, SOFTlab, James P. Morse, Dan Blackman, Hoyt L Stearns,
fablous Kate Jones and of course let's not forget Mario and Company

WHAT I USE PAPER FOR

██████████████████████

Loz Ives
Because Studio
Preston, England

Paper plays a huge role in my job. That may seem obvious, since I'm a graphic designer, but it really does.

I take notes in meetings; scribble ideas down in the endless supply of notepads I own; sketch ideas for logos, grids, layouts, and typefaces. I write obsessive to-do lists that are then edited relentlessly until there is no space left on the page. I even just fill pages with doodles when I'm on a call or tired of looking at my screen.

Paper gives me an instant outlet for my thoughts and ideas—something that, in my opinion, computers still can't match.

The rise of digital formats has naturally meant a decrease in the amount of print I actually design, so when I do get the chance, I see it as an opportunity to create something beautiful and lasting.

Therefore, my challenge as a designer is to make sure whatever I produce is a carefully considered, well-crafted piece of work that will stand the test of time.

A big part of my design is simplicity. If something doesn't need to be there, it won't be there. Paper plays a large role in this, adding so much to the work I produce. I rely on the stocks and different finishes to add a tone to my design work.

Rather than it being an afterthought, deciding which paper stock to use is the first thing I think about when starting a job. I consider how the printed piece will look when it's finished before I even make a mark on the screen. By thinking about the end format first, it informs the way I then approach the entire design process.

A good example of this would be the identity project for interior design company, Tilt (see page 90). At its core, the logo is a very simple, styled typeface with a blue color scheme. But for the printed materials, a metallic blue foil was combined with a recycled gray board stock to give the brand much more depth, showing the two sides to their own work—the clean architectural crispness in the foil, and the earthy, textured, environmentally focused gray board.

Paper gives design personality and it's something I try and play on in all the work I produce.

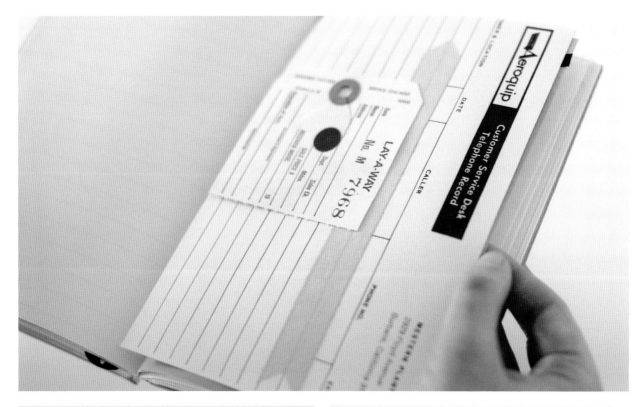

Margot Harrington   USA

Brandcentral USA

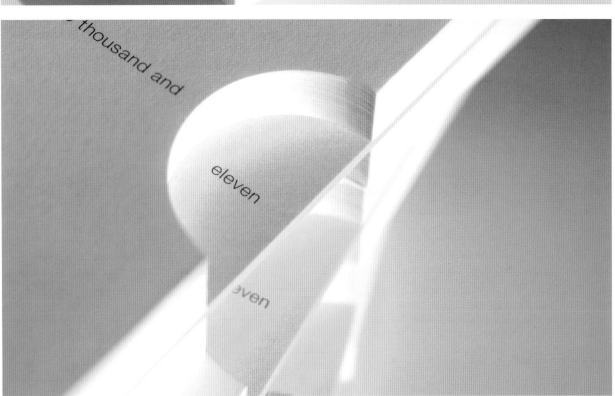

Matter Strategic Design USA

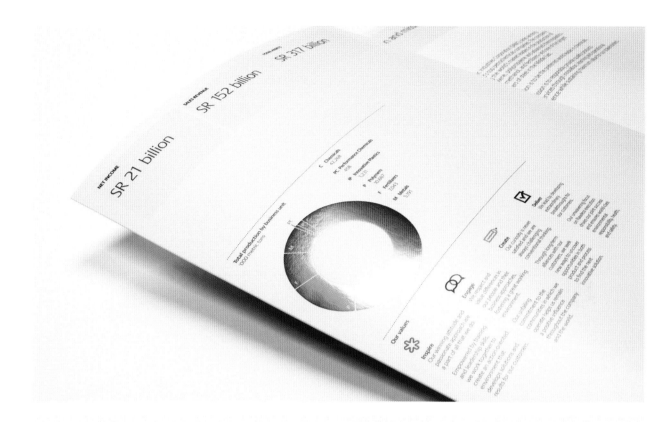

Bisqit   England

Lovestain Graphica   Belgium

Brogen Averill New Zealand

Brigada Creativa   Spain

Blok

Canada

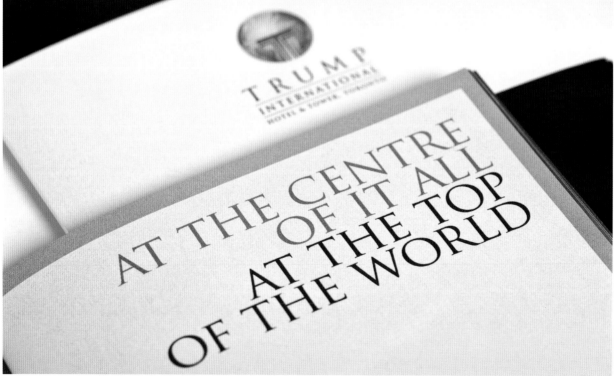

Zync Canada

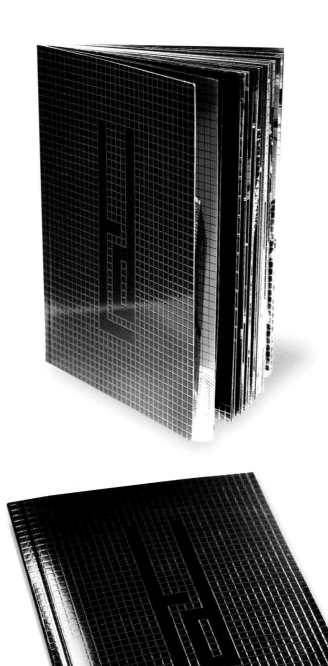

Mirko Ilić   USA

Foundry Communications   Canada

PER·SE·VER·ANCE:
NOUN. STEADY
PERSISTENCE IN A
COURSE OF ACTION,
A PURPOSE, A STATE,
ETC., ESPECIALLY IN
SPITE OF DIFFICULTIES
OR OBSTACLES.

SEE ALSO;
CELTIC EXPLORATION.

Foundry Communications Canada

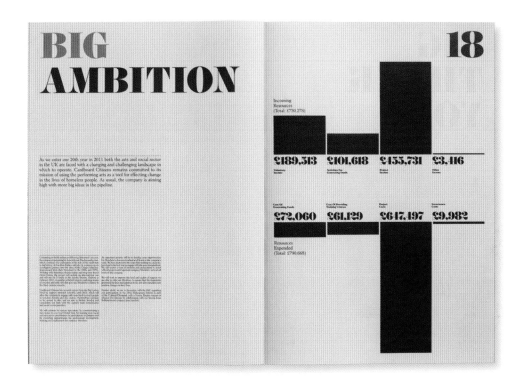

The tissue paper used to enclose the booklet is a playful reference to the line "We Are Fashion Catchers."

WE ARE FASHION
CATCHERS

CLOSER LOOK

Chevychase
Sweden

A lookbook for the autumn 2009 collection for clothing brand Human Scales.

The scale pattern used in tags, labels, and other collateral is a great detail.

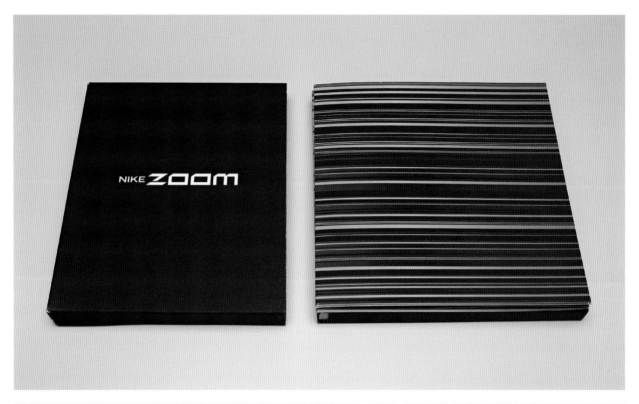

Plazm USA

EIGA Design   Germany

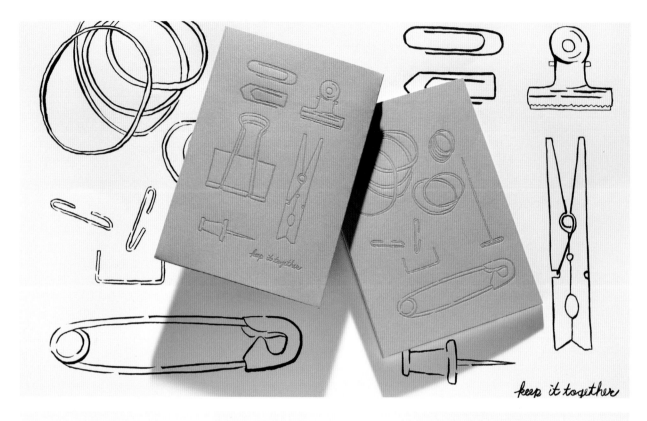

Lilco Letterpress USA

Square Feet Design USA

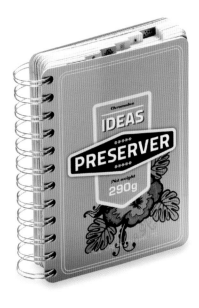

Zinnobergruen   Germany

RoAndCo Studio   USA

girl walk //
all day

a music
video of
epic
proportions

Kelli Anderson   USA

**STEVE WYNN'S
YARD DOG
SPRING
TRAINING
★ 2011 ★**

**STEVE WYNN + THE MIRACLE 3
THE BASEBALL PROJECT**
THE MINUS 5   JON LANGFORD & SKULL ORCHARD
THE AUTUMN DEFENSE   MARK EITZEL   ELEVENTH DREAM DAY
CASEY NEILL & THE NORWAY RATS   THE SLUMMERS   CALIBRO 35
SATURDAY   MARCH 19   NOON 'TIL SEVEN AT YARD DOG

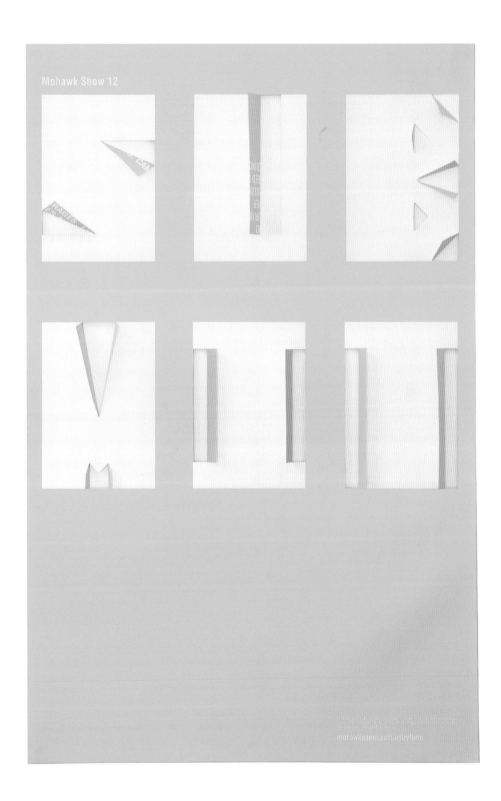

Tether USA

Bureau of Betterment   USA

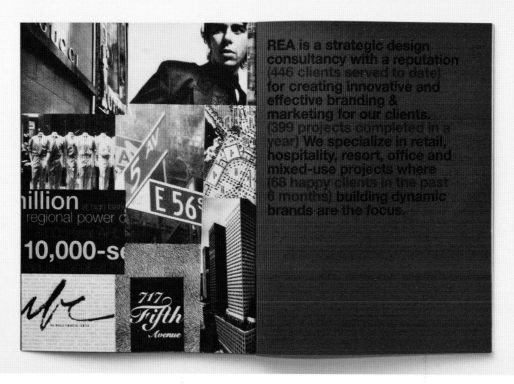

Real Estate Arts USA

Real Estate Arts USA

PACKAGING

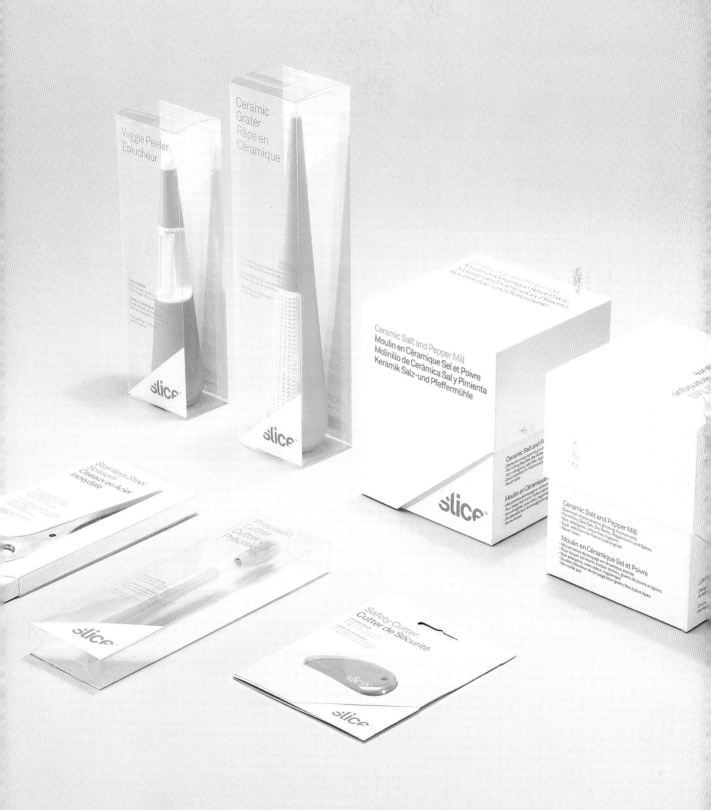

Veggie Peeler
Éplucheur

Ceramic
Grater
Râpe en
Céramique

slice™

slice™

Ceramic Salt and Pepper Mill
Moulin en Céramique Sel et Poivre
Molinillo de Cerámica Sal y Pimienta
Keramik Salz-und Pfeffermühle

slice™

Stainless Steel
Scissors
Ciseaux en Acier
Inoxydé

Precision
Cutter
Cutter de
Précision

slice™

Safety Cutter
Cutter de Sécurité

slice™

Ceramic Salt and Pepper Mill
Moulin en Céramique Sel et Poivre

TAKING STOCK OF YOUR PAPER CHOICES

Roanne Adams
RoAndCo Studio
New York, New York

When my team and I approach a print project, we put our energy into every detail, considering not only the physical form of the piece but the sum of all of its parts—i.e., the graphics, the paper stock, the printing technique, the quantity needed, the budget allotted, and so on.

Learning what paper stocks work best with what printing techniques is an art in itself. For example, you can't offset print on certain paper stocks, and there are certain papers that work best with letterpress and silk screening. Creating print pieces can become a bit of a puzzle, but once all the pieces are in place, it can be very rewarding.

We feel it's important to choose paper stocks that further convey the idea of the design piece. The choice to go with one paper stock or another should always be based on the concept and relate back to the brand we are creating it for. We always ask ourselves, "What's the message we are trying to send to this audience?"

Texture, thickness, quality, or lack there of, are all characteristics of paper that we think about before going to print. We choose the paper stock with the same careful consideration we would give to choosing a typeface. For example, the decision to go with a Kraft stock over a high-gloss coated stock is an intentional decision that conveys a mood as well as a tactile feeling.

Consistency is something we strive for when working with a long-term client's brand. We typically assign a certain paper stock to their brand style guide. That's not to say we don't often use other paper stocks to diversify the branding, but we only do so with an intentional reason.

We tend to stick with the same paper stock for brands the same way we tend to use a consistent typeface, treating it as another tool in the brand package to help tell the brand story and build up brand recognition.

Pinpointing what is most important when choosing a paper stock is key. Is it the color, the texture, the price? What's best suited for the chosen printing technique? Or something even more specific like, is it 100 percent recycled?

If color is key and needs to match a certain Pantone, you might be out of luck because paper colors are becoming less and less available. You might want to consider choosing the paper stock color first and then choosing the Pantone ink color. For colored papers, we tend to go with a French paper or Wausau.

If letterpress is the chosen printing technique, then we typically like to go with a softer, more impressionable "art paper." Art paper can be defined as high-quality paper with a texture that only a printing technique like letterpress or silk screening can handle. This is by no means the type of paper you can run through an offset press. There is a certain human touch to art paper, and letterpress printing is a manual technique with quality results that are unparalleled to that of a machine.

The array of choices and technicalities in print are an asset to any designer's knowledge base. My team and I always strive to explore the best possible options for the desired brand message with any print-involved task. It is the finer details that can affect the outcome of a project and ultimately influence the way a brand is perceived.

Modern 8   USA

Mash Australia

Antti Kangas   Finland

Matadog Design   USA

Hatch Design USA

Hatch Design   USA

LOVELY HONEY

Jamie Nash   USA

CLOSER LOOK

The Metric System Design Studio

Norway

The identity for Illegal Burger, Oslo's newest
and finest burger joint.

Materials were chosen for
almost immediate disposal, but
the variety of design elements
and smart use of stamps and
stickers ensure the identity
doesn't feel that way.

Burgers are wrapped in a
patterned paper made up of a
variety of burger characters. This
paper contrasts nicely with the
bare kraft materials used for the
bag and box.

Stickers featuring various characters seal the boxes.

HAMBURGERFONTS
ABCDEFGHIJKLMNO
12345670
Hamburgerfonts
abcdefghijklmno
12345670

HAMBURGERFONTS
ABCDEFGHIJKLMNO
12345670
Hamburgerfonts
abcdefghijklmno
12345670

HAMBURGERFONTS
ABCDEFGHIJKLMNO
12345670
Hamburgerfonts
abcdefghijklmno
12345670

HAMBURGERFONTS
ABCDEFGHIJKLMNO
12345670
Hamburgerfonts
abcdefghijklmno
12345670

Think packaging   USA

Kutchibok   England

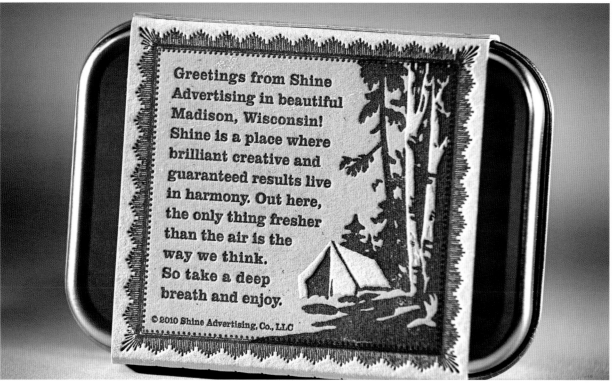

Shine Advertising   Australia

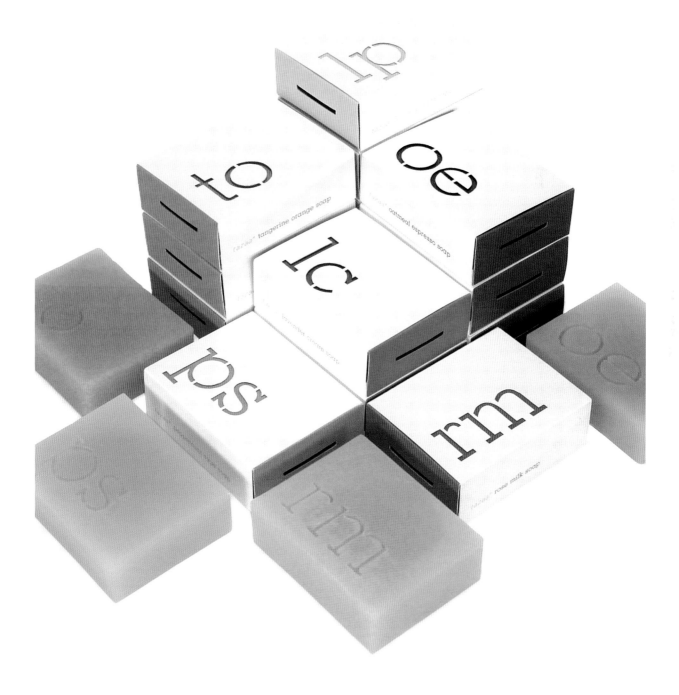

Hatch Design USA

CLOSER LOOK

JJAAKK

USA

Packaging and logo design for Melt,
a gourmet chocolate shop.

Characteristics of melted chocolate
were used throughout the packaging.

The clean, white base helps elevate
the other colors and seems to even
resemble white chocolate.

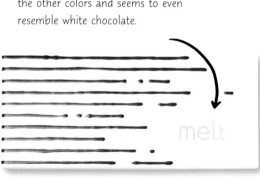

The gold sticker appears to
be melting as well.

Johann Hierholzer   Finland

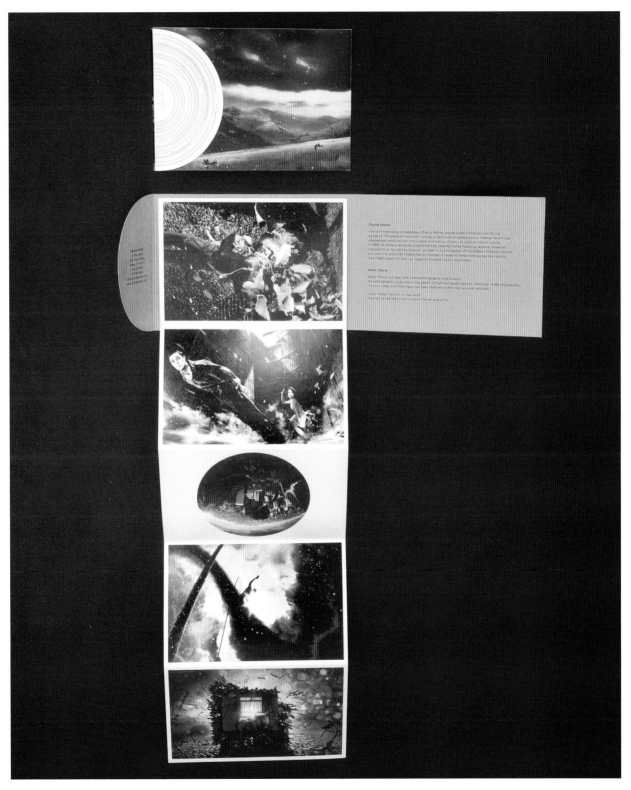

Mirko Ilić USA

Plazm   USA

Interabang England

Politanski Design Poland

Politanski Design Poland

Plazm   USA

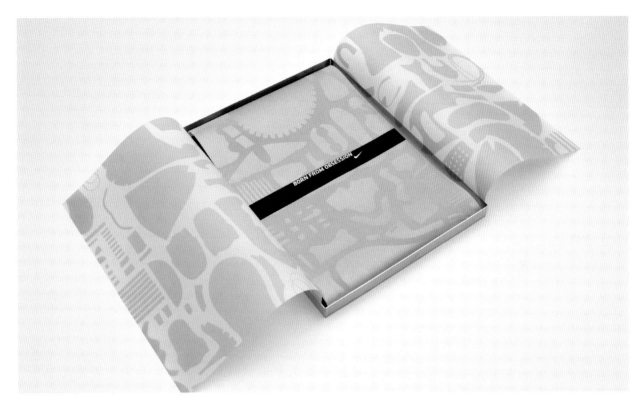

Plazm   USA

Zync   USA

Julie VonDerVellen   USA

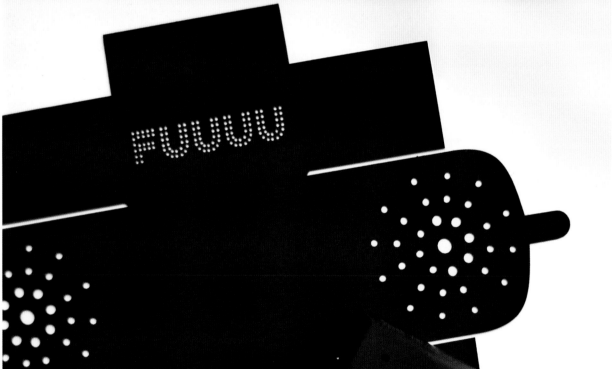

Kelli Anderson   USA

CLOSER LOOK

Manual

USA

Slice collaborates with world-renowned designers such as Yves Behar and Karim Rashid to create award-winning ceramic cutting tools for the home and office.

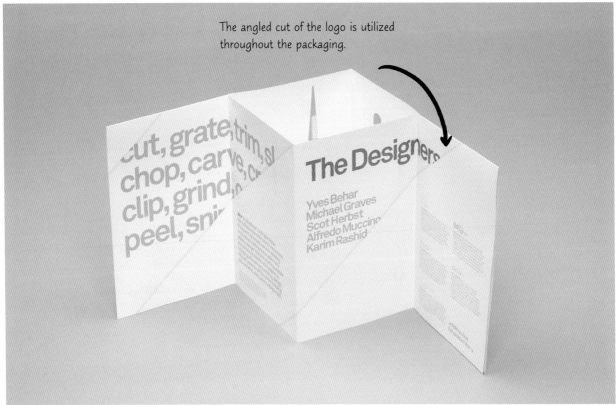

The angled cut of the logo is utilized throughout the packaging.

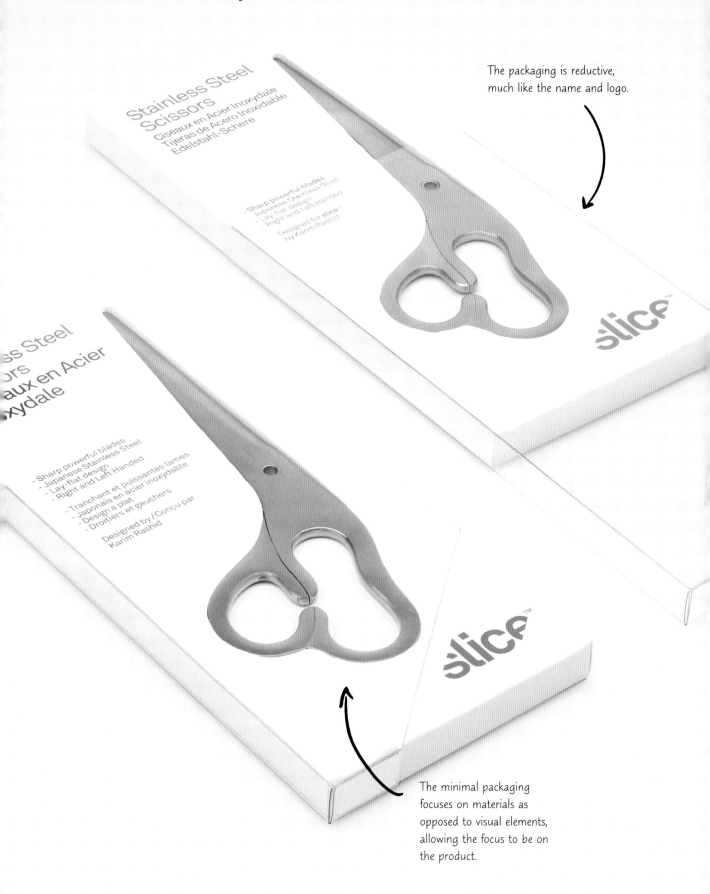

The packaging is reductive, much like the name and logo.

Stainless Steel
Scissors
Ciseaux en Acier Inoxydale
Tijeras de Acero Inoxidable
Edelstahl-Schere

- Sharp powerful blades
- Japanese Stainless Steel
- Lay-flat design
- Right and Left Handed

Designed for slice™
by Karim Rashid

ss Steel
ors
aux en Acier
xydale

- Sharp powerful blades
- Japanese Stainless Steel
- Lay-flat design
- Right and Left Handed

- Tranchant et puissantes lames
- Japonais en acier inoxydable
- Design a plat
- Droitiers et gauchers

Designed by / Conçu par
Karim Rashid

slice™

slice™

The minimal packaging focuses on materials as opposed to visual elements, allowing the focus to be on the product.

Zinnobergruen   Germany

Brogen Averill   New Zealand

Chris DeLorenzo USA

Tad Carpenter Creative   USA

CLOSER LOOK

Plazm
USA

Formerly Vinton Studios, LAIKA does animation for the commercial and entertainment industries. This package is the first DVD release for LAIKA's commercial division.

There's a nice revealing element as a result of the difference between the exterior and the contents.

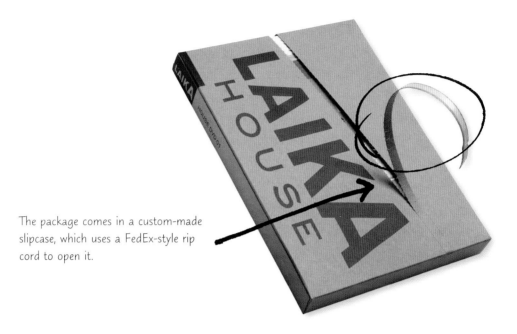

The package comes in a custom-made slipcase, which uses a FedEx-style rip cord to open it.

The slipcase angle mimics the top edge of the logo.

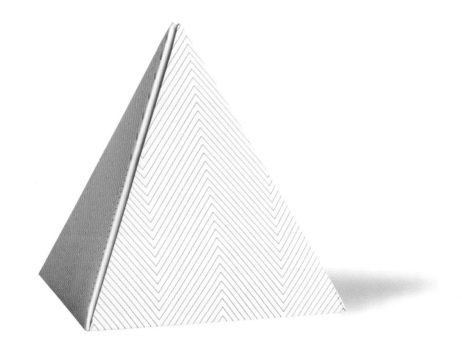

RoAndCo Studio   USA

RoAndCo Studio   USA

Base Design   USA

Un jour de bonheur
mais différent…
GRAANMARKT 13

Base Design   USA

CARDS & INVITATIONS

Michelle Maguire   USA

PLEASE JOIN US

THIS SPACE FOR WRITING MESSAGES

POST CARD

R S V P
KINDLY REPLY BY
AUGUST 1ST

YES YES YES ** NO NO NO
NAME
OF GUESTS IN YOUR PARTY

MICHELLE MAGU
AND AARON BE

1758 KING AVE
COLUMBUS OH
4 3 2 1 2

PUBLISHED BY ASHEVILLE POST CARD CO., ASHEVILLE, N. C.

COME HUNGRY
DRESS TO KILL

THE HIDDEN TALENTS OF ORDINARY THINGS

Kelli Anderson
New York, New York

More blank than the proverbial "blank canvas" is the humble piece of paper. Paper is the substrate for Einstein's Special Theory of Relativity and also holds in the greasy glut of a McDonald's cheeseburger. It spans the gamut of human experience.

Paper is also painfully ordinary as a medium. Devoid of inherent inspiration, the blank piece of paper is verbal shorthand for creative block. However, a material this commonplace can be a creative ally precisely because of its ho-hum familiarity. Paper possesses quotidian street cred—everyone knows how it is supposed to function, and yet, it has hidden talents that lie dormant. Its unsuspecting demeanor hides the potential for radical degrees of interpretation. A piece of paper can grow up to become an interactive game, a four-dimensional flexographic animation, a fortune teller, a legitimate document of truth, or a convincing counterfeit. The possibilities are as vast as they are humbling.

My work oftentimes feels like a hunt for unrealized meaning in tired forms. This pursuit requires an exploration of avenues that initially appear to be dead ends ... like wedding invitations. For me, they have always seemed like empty cultural obligations, often exposing precisely what the couple would prefer to leave hidden: conspicuous consumption, showy one-upmanship, empty sentimentality, and the effacement of individual identity. However, I do love working on paper projects and—as it turns out—friends frequently request that I make their invitations.

Thus, these projects begin with a rebellious attitude: How can we "un-wedding invitation" this wedding invitation? Where is the actual meaning and sentiment hiding? In the vast and chaotic universe, what brought us all together as friends in the first place? Can that ineffable thing be extracted, distilled, and folded into paper somehow?

Miraculously, after days of searching, a strategy emerges for bottling that essence. I solicit feedback, which almost always amounts to, "That would be cool, but it would never work." These words inspire a flurry of action: calling suppliers, impersonating a much larger design firm, getting samples, testing, taping, mocking up, getting more samples, and hitting wooden surfaces frequently. It's always a lot of work, but as long as the concept was sound, the project comes together as if it were inevitable. My favorite projects simultaneously yield something unexpected (but demonstrable) about the medium of paper—and something surprising (but true) about our shared curiosity.

Mélangerie Inc.   USA

J Fletcher Design   USA

Mélangerie Inc. USA

Kathy Mueller Graphic Design USA

Mélangerie Inc.   USA

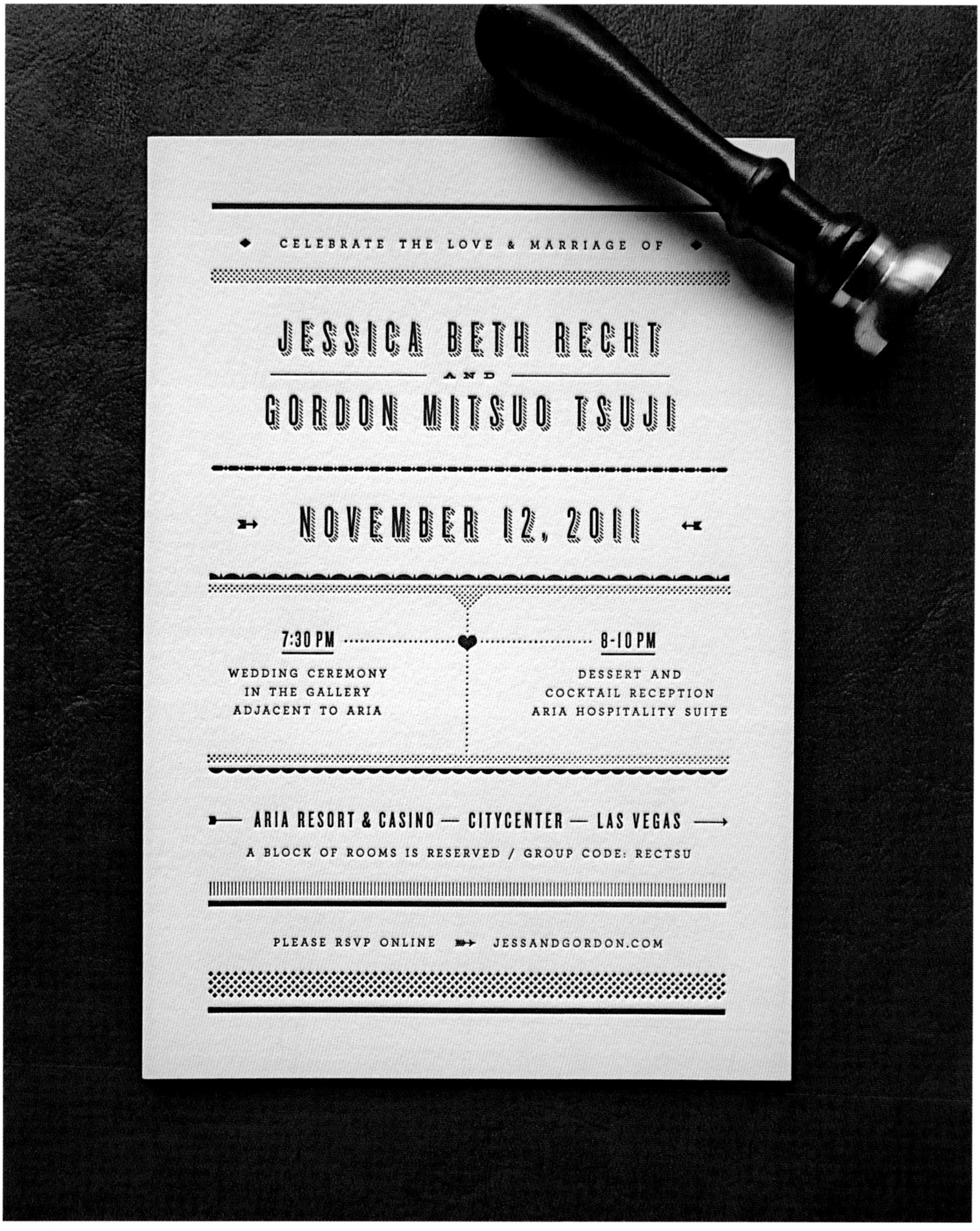

◆ CELEBRATE THE LOVE & MARRIAGE OF ◆

JESSICA BETH RECHT
AND
GORDON MITSUO TSUJI

NOVEMBER 12, 2011

7:30 PM ◆ **8-10 PM**

WEDDING CEREMONY
IN THE GALLERY
ADJACENT TO ARIA

DESSERT AND
COCKTAIL RECEPTION
ARIA HOSPITALITY SUITE

► ARIA RESORT & CASINO — CITYCENTER — LAS VEGAS →

A BLOCK OF ROOMS IS RESERVED / GROUP CODE: RECTSU

PLEASE RSVP ONLINE ➤➤ JESSANDGORDON.COM

Brandon Kirk Design USA

CLOSER LOOK

Kelli Anderson
USA

When folded just so, this card turns into a manually spun paper record player that plays an "invitation song" recorded by the bride and groom. The clear flexidisc is foil-stamped with a partial rendering of the couple, so that when turned, it reveals four stages in the couple's life. The whole package is contained within an op-art/record groove cover with a wraparound letterpressed band with tear-off RSVP postcard.

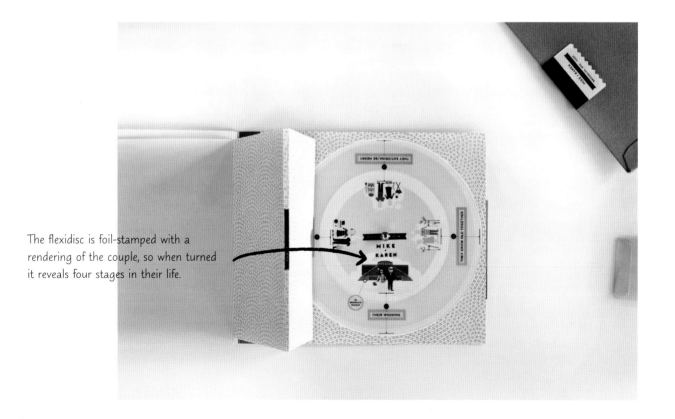

The flexidisc is foil-stamped with a rendering of the couple, so when turned it reveals four stages in their life.

The package uses a wraparound letterpressed band with a tear-off RSVP postcard.

When folded, the card turns into a manually spun paper record player.

Letterforms, Inc. USA

CRANKY PRESSMAN

NOW WITH EVEN MORE X&!#*!

2.0

FEATUR...

With some regret and a small amount of sorrow we wish to announce the end of the old Cranky Pressman website. It will cease to exist on or about the last day of September, 2009. However, reminiscent of the oft purported death of print itself, www.CrankyPressman.com will also live on in a new version 2.0. This updated incarnation will be a source for letterpress information and printing services along with other gaudy online gimmickry today's young designers expect. 'Tis a sad and flagrant jump aboard the bandwagon by a couple of old printers. Please drop by the new site to pay your respects or offer your condolences.

BUSTING OUR
NUTS FOR YOU!

BLOOD, SWEAT,
TEARS & INK.

PAPER?
YES INDEED.

OPERATORS ARE STANDING BY
1-800-433-1288

LOL! OMG! WTF! ETC! WE ARE ON THE INTERWEBS
WWW.CRANKYPRESSMAN.COM

FOLLOW US:
@CRANKYPRESSMAN

PRINTED ON CLASSIC NATURAL 130# COVER STOCK. DESIGN & ILLUSTRATION: WWW.MIKEYBURTON.COM

A division of
**The Graphic Touch
Letterpress Company.**
150 Penn Avenue
Salem, OH 44460

PRSRT STD
US Postage
PAID
Canton, OH
Permit # 1005

Mikey Burton   USA

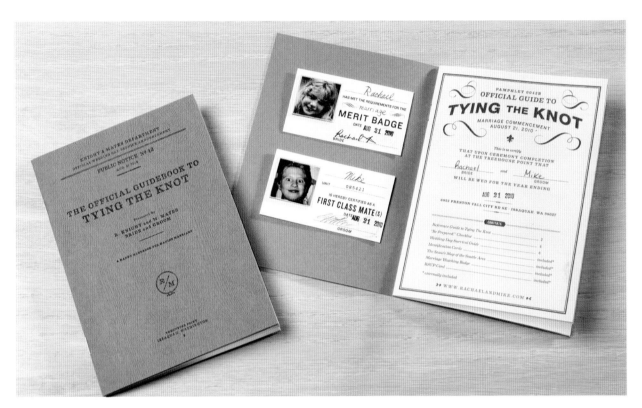

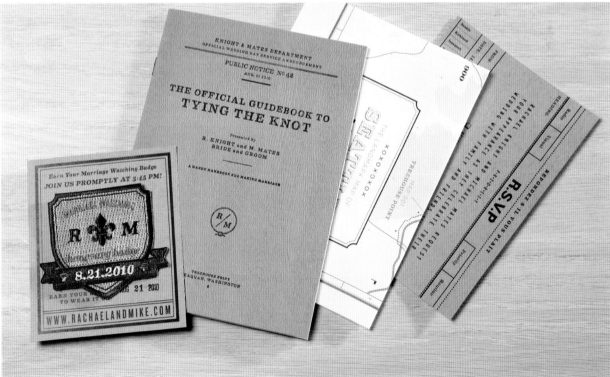

Urban Influence   USA

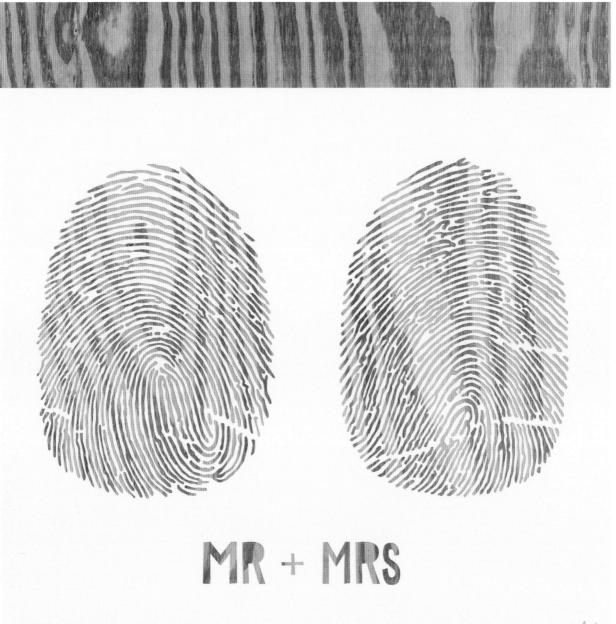

Lori Danelle   USA

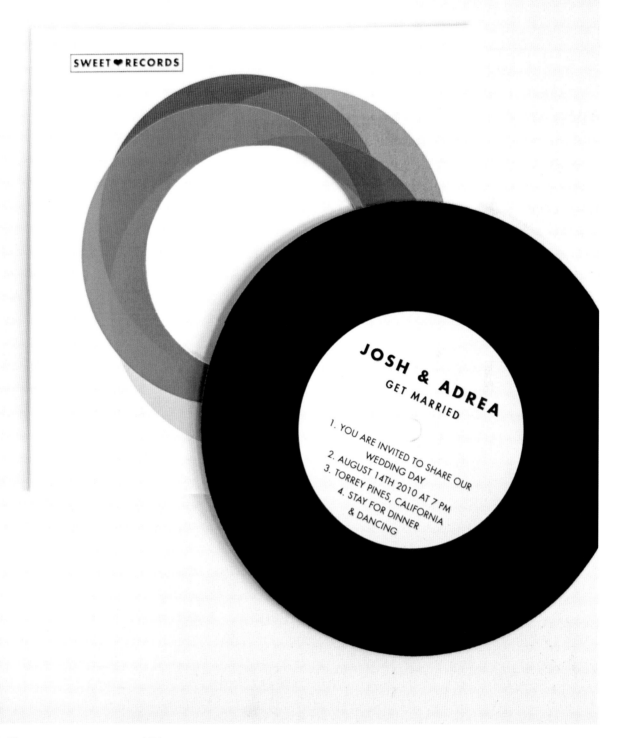

SWEET ♥ RECORDS

JOSH & ADREA
GET MARRIED

1. YOU ARE INVITED TO SHARE OUR
WEDDING DAY
2. AUGUST 14TH 2010 AT 7 PM
3. TORREY PINES, CALIFORNIA
4. STAY FOR DINNER
& DANCING

Colin Payson   USA

Amie Harrison   USA

CLOSER LOOK

FBA
USA

The Austin Film Society's annual Texas Film
Hall of Fame event honors Texans who've made
a significant contribution to filmmaking and
entertainment, as well as non-Texans who've
advanced the Texas entertainment industry.

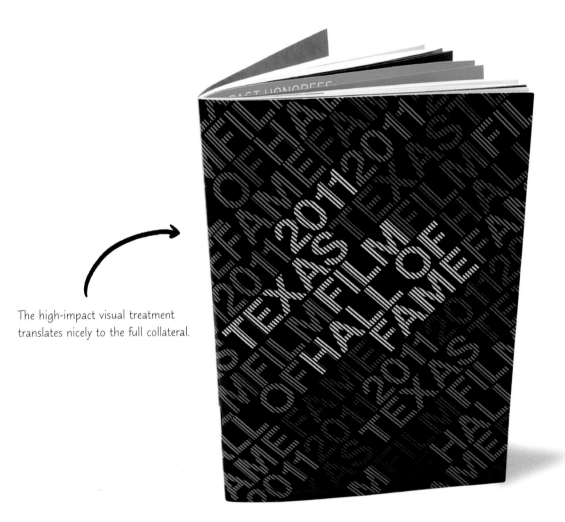

The high-impact visual treatment
translates nicely to the full collateral.

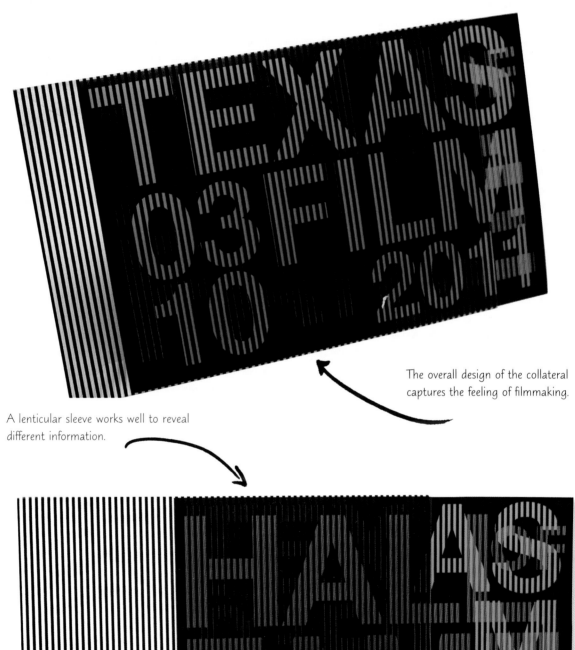

The overall design of the collateral captures the feeling of filmmaking.

A lenticular sleeve works well to reveal different information.

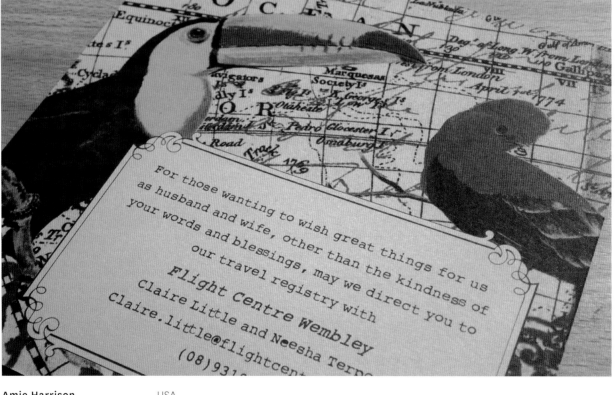

Amie Harrison   USA

Lydia Nichols   USA

Nick Brue   USA

Mohamed Axlif   Maldives

Moolee Bunnag   USA

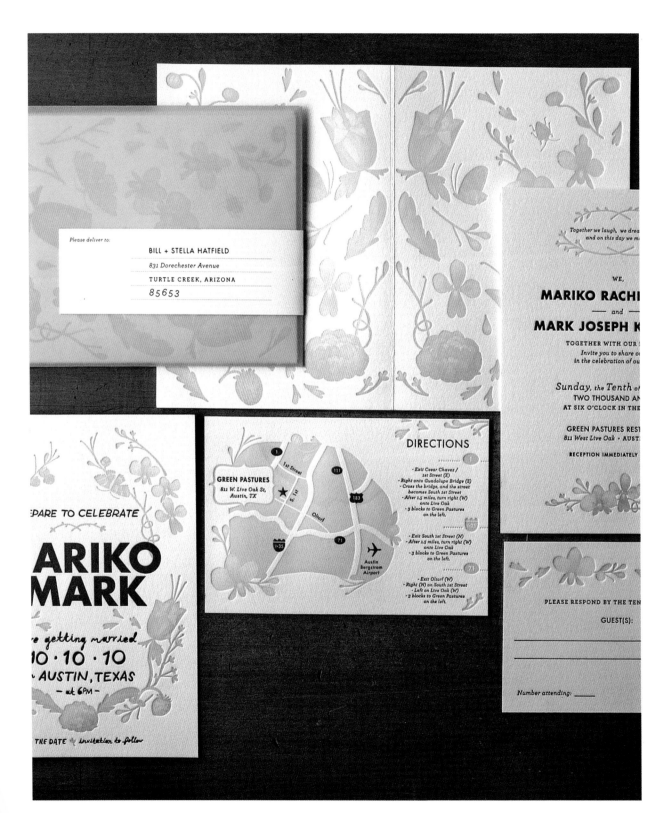

Julia Kostreva   USA

State Digital   USA

A. Micah Smith USA

Karolin Schnoor   USA

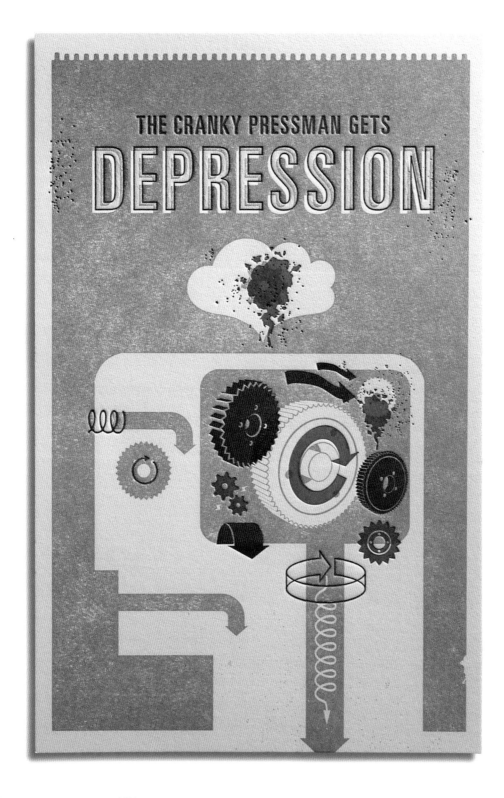

Mikey Burton USA

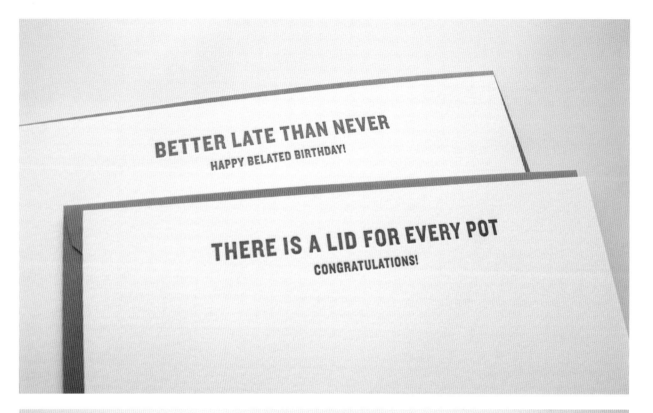

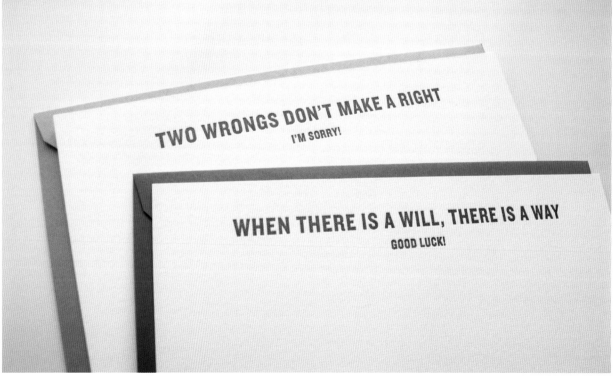

L'Office Optimiste   USA

Kanella   USA

CLOSER LOOK

Ello There
USA

Ello There is the couple/duo Maddie and
Seth Lucas. They created a foldout map
wedding invitation meant to be customized
for different clients.

An *X* marks the spot for each
client's wedding.

The warm stock and red overlaid
type work together to age the
invitation.

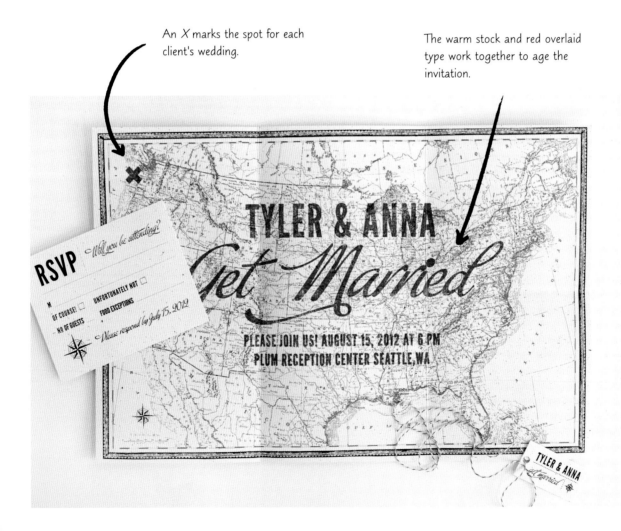

This is a great example of using
inexpensive materials in a way
that adds a level of production
and detail.

Karolin Schnoor   USA

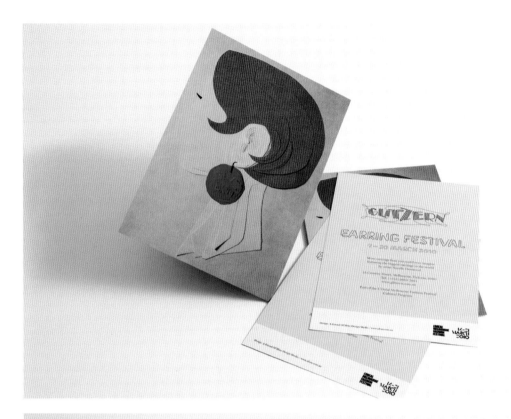

A Friend of Mine   Australia

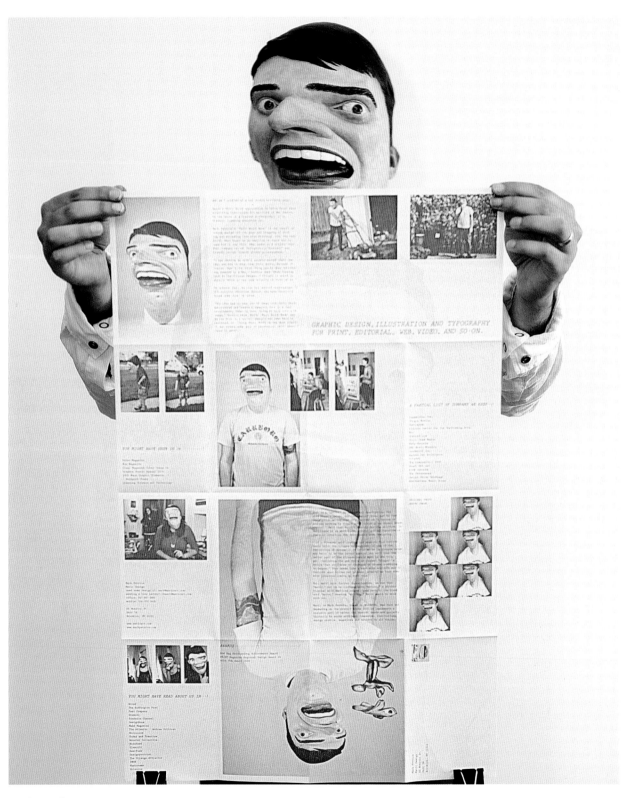

Mark Pernice   USA

Peters   USA

Natoof   United Arab Emirates

Studiotwentysix2   USA

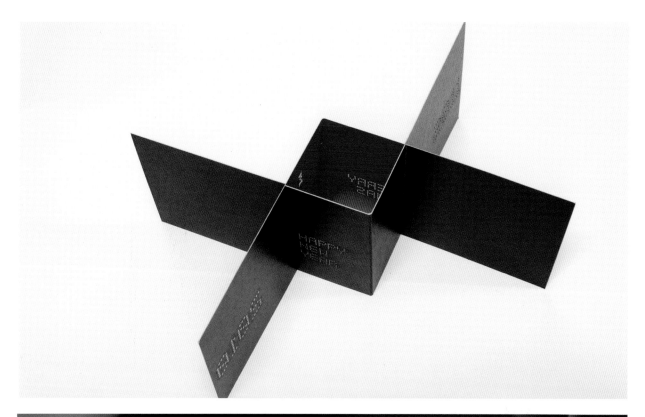

X-Sight England

B.L.A Design Company   USA

BOOKS *traditionally have edges: some are rough-cut, some are smooth-cut, and a few, at least at my extravagant publishing house, are even top-stained. In the electronic anthill, where are the edges? The book revolution, which, from the Renaissance on, taught men and women to cherish and cultivate their individuality, threatens to end in a sparkling cloud of snippets. So, booksellers, defend your lonely forts. Keep your edges dry. Your edges are our edges. For some of us, books are intrinsic to our sense of personal identity.* JOHN UPDIKE

BURKE'S BOOK STORE

Since 1875, providing Memphis with the finest selection of new, used & rare books.

936 SOUTH COOPER STREET, MEMPHIS, TENNESSEE 38104   901-278-7484   WWW.BURKESBOOKS.COM

Ithaca Typothetae   USA

Lilco Letterpress   USA

Lilco Letterpress   USA

Lilco Letterpress   USA

Natoof   United Arab Emirates

CLOSER LOOK

Nikolaus Schmidt Design
Austria

The design firm's foldout card celebrating
Christmas and the new year in 2011.

The foldout shape is a nice alternative
to the traditional card format, and the
color palette is a departure from the
usual holiday suspects.

The two sides are a study in contrast.
The pattern hides the phrase "Merry
Christmas and a Happy New Year."

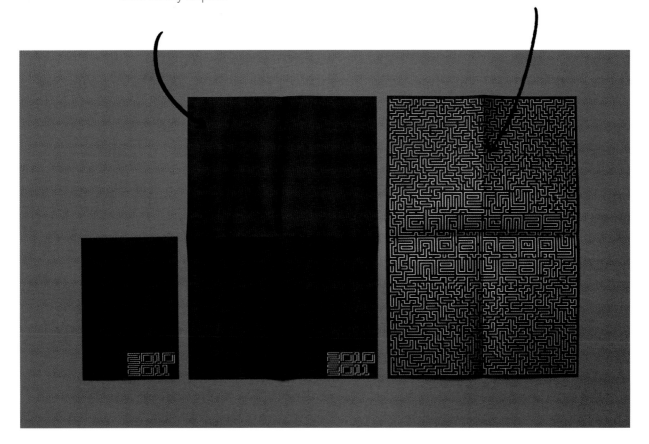

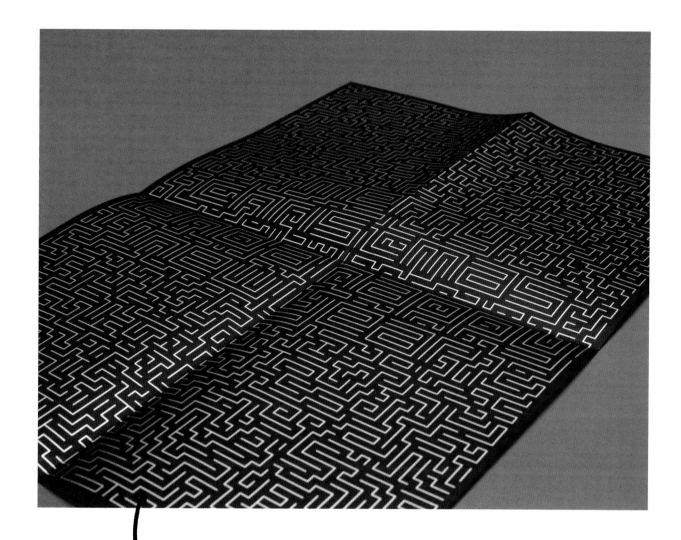

A simple concept executed well on
nice stock creates a stunning graphic.

Re: Creative   Austria

Zync   Canada

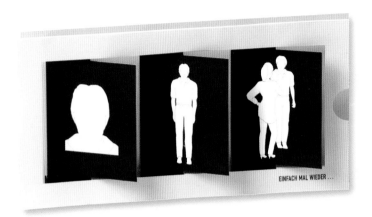

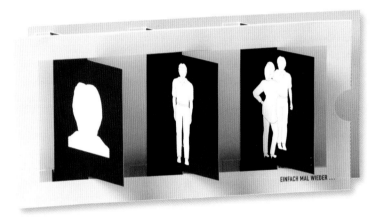

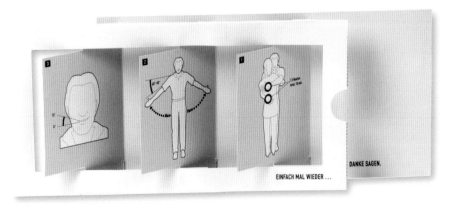

steinzeit-medien design   Germany

Steve Scott Graphic Design Australia

Tad Carpenter Creative   USA

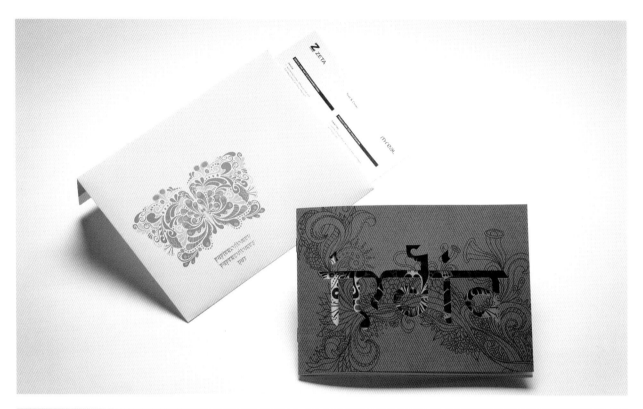

Zinnobergruen   USA

Jee-eun Lee   USA

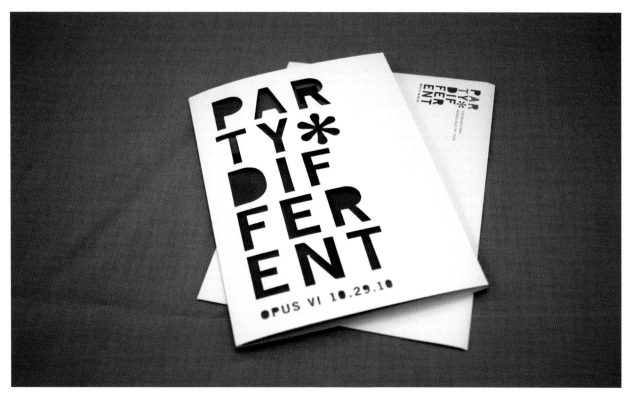

S Design Inc.   USA

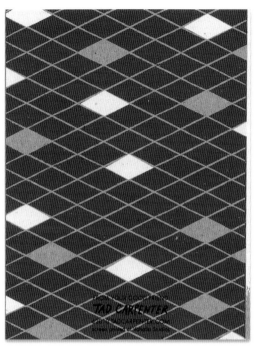

Tad Carpenter Creative   USA

Tad Carpenter Creative USA

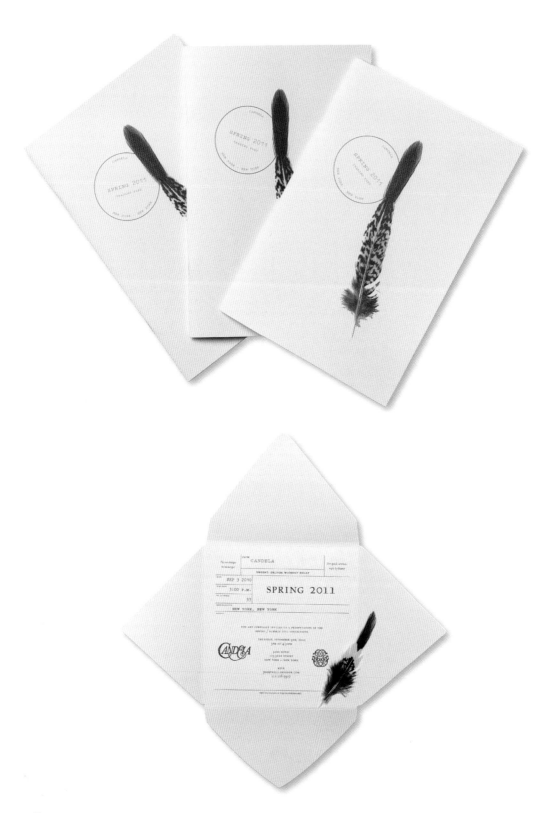

RoAndCo Studio USA

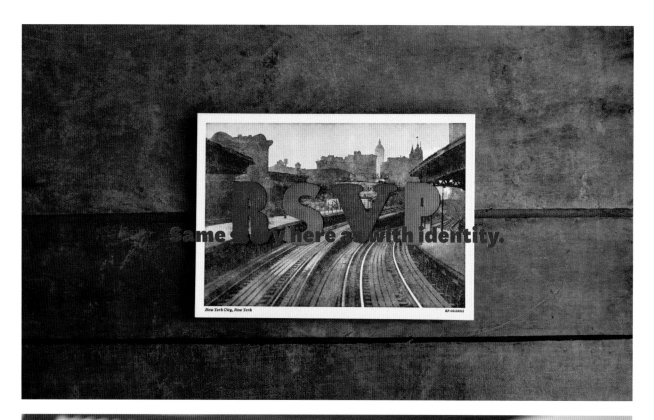

Aaron Bouvier Design USA

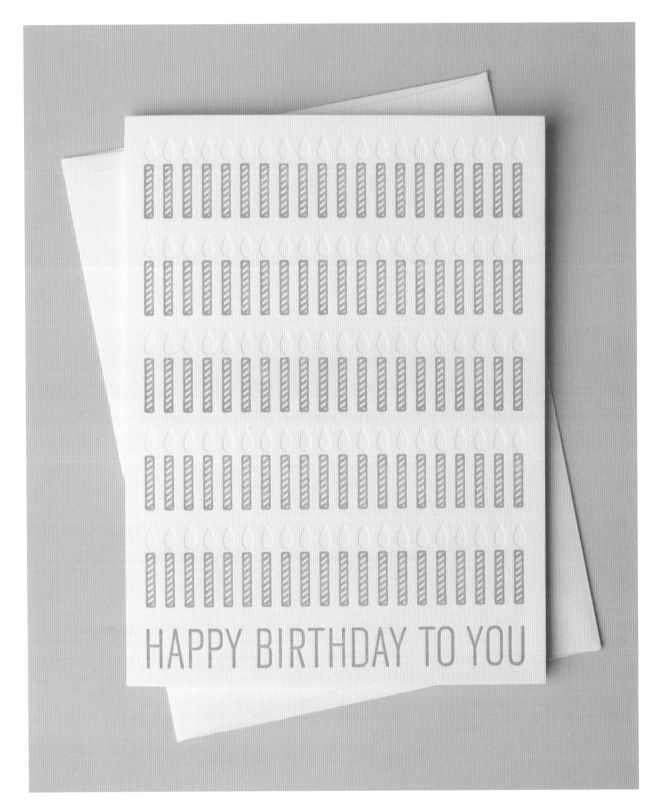

Wieden + Kennedy   USA

Product Superior　　　USA

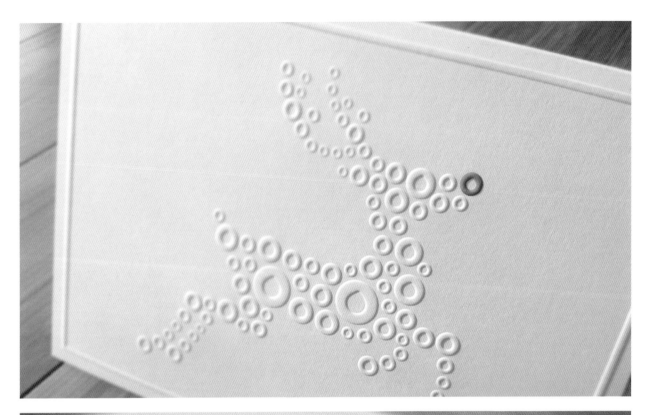

INK   USA

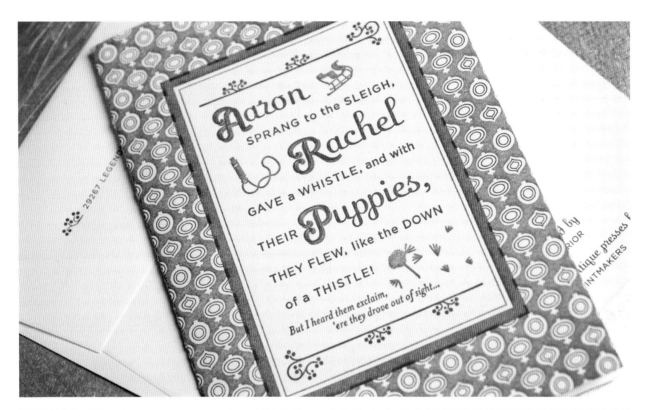

Aaron SPRANG to the SLEIGH, & Rachel GAVE a WHISTLE, and with THEIR Puppies, THEY FLEW, like the DOWN of a THISTLE! But I heard them exclaim, 'ere they drove out of sight...

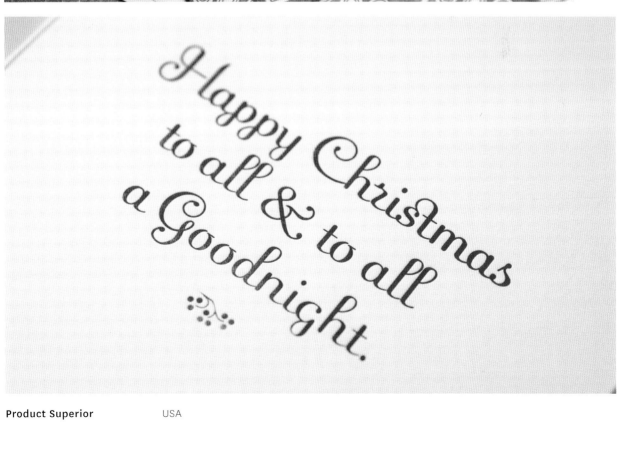

Happy Christmas to all & to all a Goodnight.

Product Superior   USA

PAPERCRAFT

Owen Gildersleeve   England

POP UP BAR

Gareth Peirc
Why al-Megrahi
is innocent, page

Don't look!
Streakers are bac
page 13

POP UP SHOP

POPUP

THIS

THAT

92

Is there no end to
the pop-up revolution?

EMBRACING IMPERFEC-TIONS

Owen Gildersleeve
London, England

My interest in tactile artwork began at school. I was fasci-nated by artists such as Anselm Kiefer, Robert Rauschenberg, and Cy Twombly, so I'd spend my art lessons trying to create works in their style. This involved lots of experimentation with different mediums and getting very messy in the pro-cess. As my school life progressed, I also had the opportunity to study photography. I would often while away my time in the darkrooms developing photos and trying out different processes. Gradually, these two interests started to combine, and this is what eventually led to the way that I work now.

Although I still work with a range of mediums, my portfolio is now predominantly filled with handcrafted paper creations. This shift in material preference first began when I was asked to create more complex artworks, which I thought would be better suited to a more versatile medium. Since then, paper has become a key material in my working practice, and there are few projects that don't involve it.

My working process has many stages from sketch to comple-tion. I normally create a round of sketches and mock-ups of my intended piece so that I can work through my ideas and figure out how I want the illustration to be assembled. Then I start making the piece. Although the illustration is based on the sketches, I still experiment quite a bit during this stage, playing with the forms and composition. Finally, I'll either photograph the finished illustration myself or work with a photographer for more complex projects. If I do the photography myself, I also take charge of the editing and retouching. This process is usually quite laborious but also very satisfying because it's nice to see a project right through to the end.

As much as I enjoy my work, it still has its downfalls. It can be very time consuming and involves a lot of patience, which is sometimes hard to maintain when I'm busy. You also really have to learn to embrace the flaws and imperfections, which can be difficult if you're a bit of a perfectionist like me. But it is these small challenges that really make me excited about the work I do, and when things finally start to come together, it definitely feels like it's all worthwhile.

Owen Gildersleeve   England

Man vs Ink   USA

Bureau of Betterment   USA

Owen Gildersleeve   England

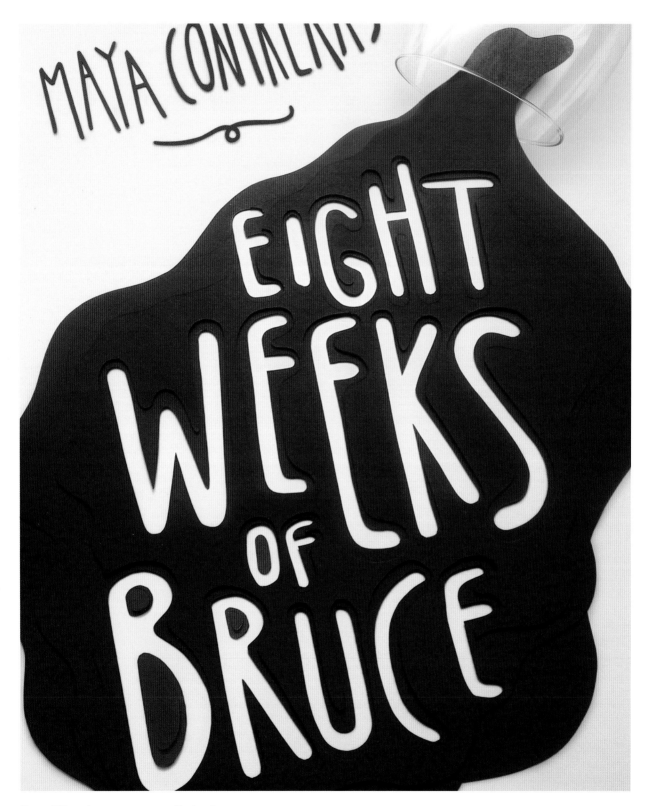

Owen Gilversleeve   England

Jeremy Slagle Graphic Design USA

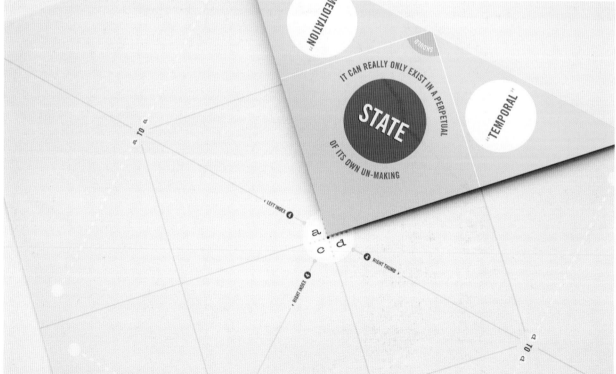

Kelli Anderson   USA

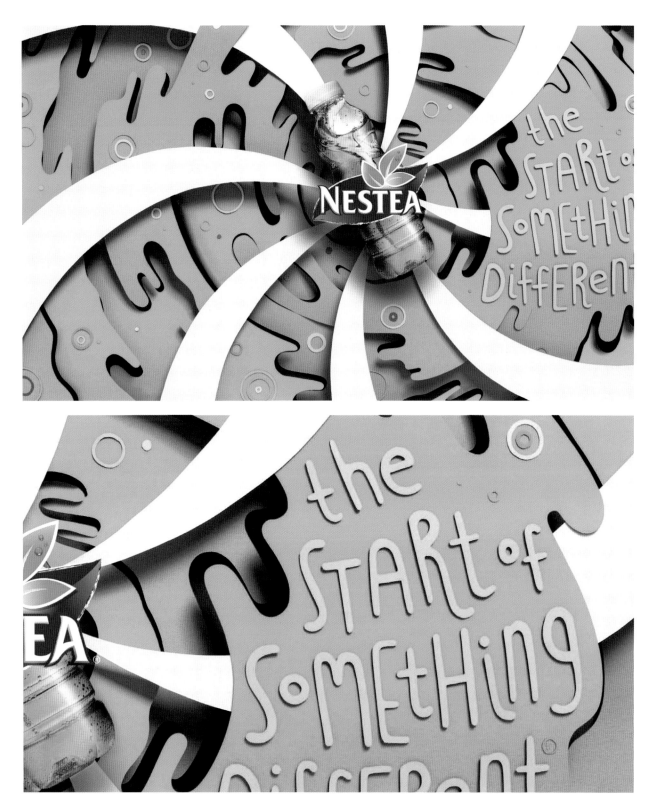

Owen Gildersleeve   England

CLOSER LOOK

Owen Gildersleeve

England

A two-part illustration for *Scientific American* to accompany the feature article "How We Are Evolving."

Each puzzle piece, all cut by hand, fits in the paper-made recess.

An incredible level of intricacy and detail is necessary to pull off something like this.

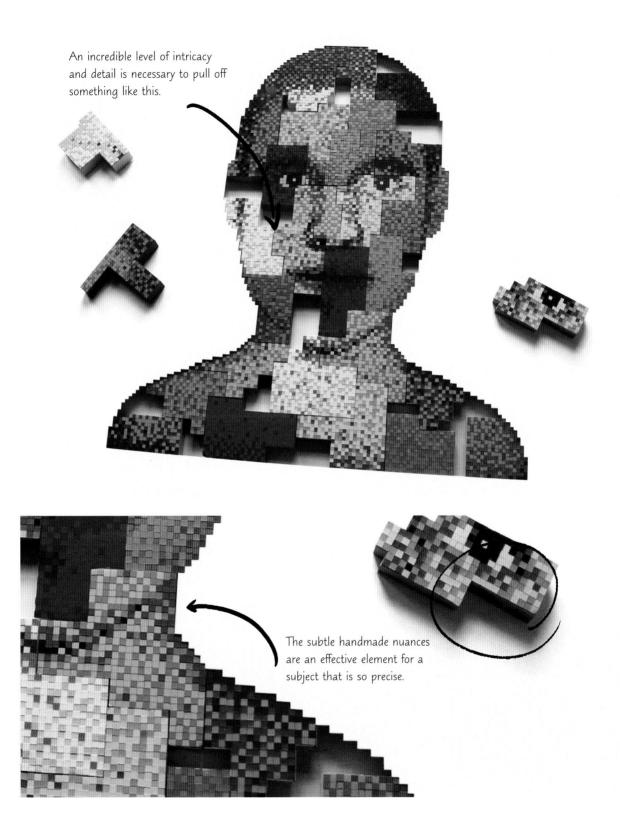

The subtle handmade nuances are an effective element for a subject that is so precise.

Tad Carpenter Creative   USA

Michéle Brummer-Everett   USA

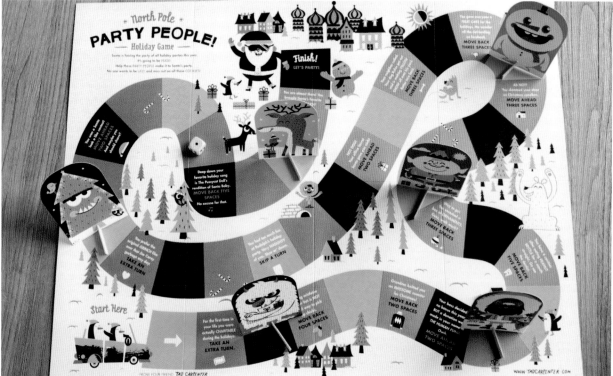

Tad Carpenter Creative   USA

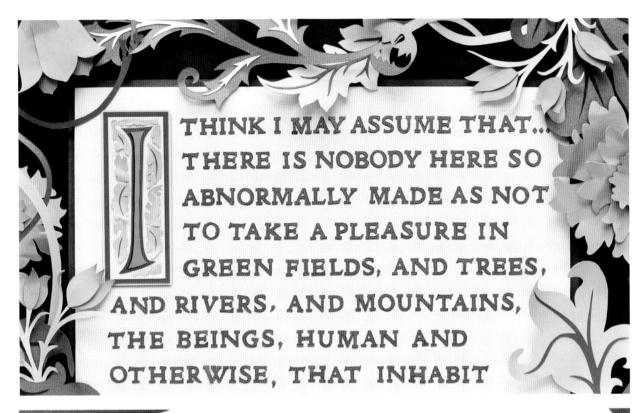

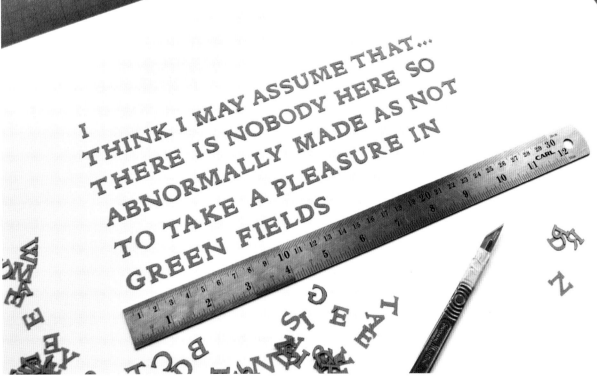

Owen Gildersleeve   England

CLOSER LOOK

A Friend of Mine

Australia

The VCE Season of Excellence, by the Victorian Curriculum and Assessment Authority (VCAA), is a series of events and exhibitions celebrating a selection of A+ grade work produced by VCE students in an array of creative fields.

Each diorama consists of a series of individual layers cut from various paper stocks. This setup makes for easier adjustment to the various layers.

The accompanying typography, which was also cut out, works well with each image

Covers for all collateral utilize the dioramas in an impactful way, leaving a lot of white space to focus on the depth of the imagery.

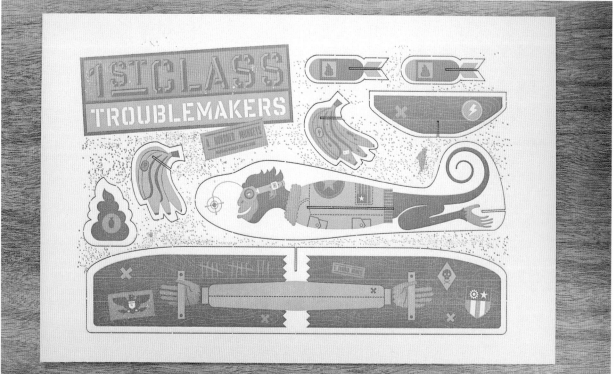

Mikey Burton   USA

Alex Robbins Germany

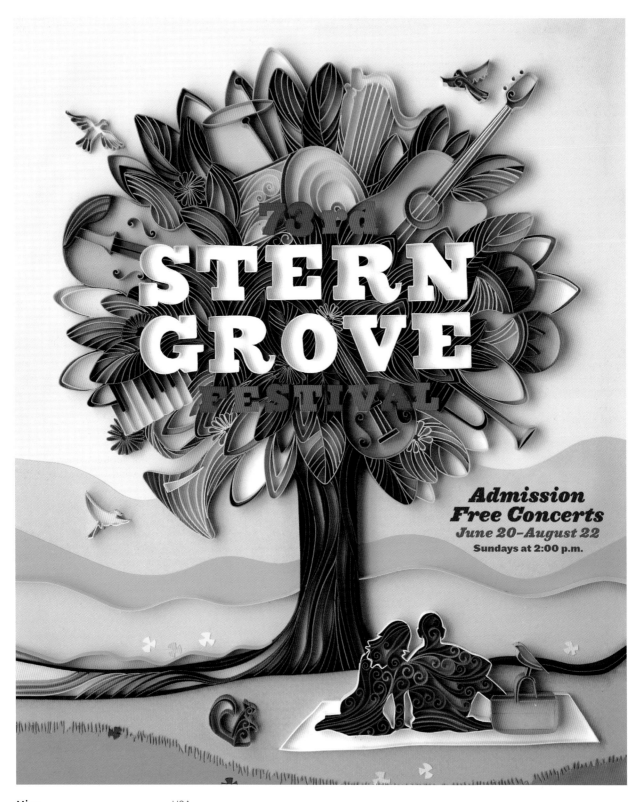

Contributors

Aaron Bouvier Design
aaronbouvier.com

Aaron Deckler
lolight.com

Aesthetic Movement
aestheticmovement.com

Agoodid
agoodid.se

Alex Robbins
alexrobbins.co.uk

A. Micah Smith
amicahsmith.com

Amie Harrison
amieharrison.com

Antti Kangas
anttikangas.fi

Base Design
basedesign.com

BBDO Designworks
bbdo.com

Because Studio
becausestudio.co.uk

Bisqit
bisqit.co.uk

B.L.A Design Company
blahdesign.com

Blok
blokdesign.com

Bond Creative Agency
bond-agency.com

Brand Agent
brand-agent.com

Brandcentral
brandcentral.ie

Brandon Kirk
brandonkirkdesign.com

Brigada Creativa
brigadacreativa.com

Brogen Averill
brogenaverill.com

Brown & White Creative
brownandwhitecreative.com

Bureau of Betterment
bureauofbetterment.com

Cassie Hester
cassiehester.com

Chevychase
chevychase.se

Chris DeLorenzo
chrisdelorenzo.com

Colin Payson
colinpayson.com

Creative Suitcase
creativesuitcase.com

The Consult
theconsult.com

Departement
departement.ca

Departures
departuresdesign.com

design8days
design8days.com

DUO
duomatic.ca

EIGA Design
eiga.de

Eight Hour Day
eighthourday.com

Ello There
ellothere.com

Fabio Ongarato Design
fabioongarato.com.au

FBA
foxtrotbravoalpha.com

Föda Studio
fodastudio.com

Foreign Policy
foreignpolicydesign.com

Foundry Communications
foundrycommunications.ca

A Friend of Mine
afom.com.au

Fuzzco
fuzzco.com

Hatch Design
hatchsf.com

Hello Tenfold
hellotenfold.com

Heydays
heydays.info

Ink
ink-la.com

Interabang
interabang.uk.com

Ithaca Typothetae
ithacatype.com

James Prunean
jamesprunean.com

Jamie Nash
jamienashillustration.
blogspot.com

Javas Lehn Studio
javaslehn.com

Jee-eun Lee Studio
jeenaya.com

Jeremy Slagle
jeremyslagle.com

Jessica Vollendorf
manvsink.com

J Fletcher Design
jfletcherdesign.com

JJAAKK
jjaakk.com

Johann Hierholzer
johann-hierholzer.com

Judith Augustin
judith-augustin.de

Julia Kostreva
juliakostreva.com

Julie VonDerVellen
julievondervellen.com

Kanella
kanella.com

Karolin Schnoor
karolinschnoor.com

Kathy Mueller
Graphic Design
muelldesign.com

Kelli Anderson
kellianderson.com

Kutchibok
kucthibok.co.uk

Letterform, Inc.
letterform.net

Lilco Letterpress
lilcoletterpress.com

Lori Danelle
loridanelle.com

Lovestain Graphica
lovestain.be

Lundgren + Lindqvist
lundgrenlindqvist.se

Lydia Nichols
lydianichols.com

Mami Awamura
mamiawamura.com

Man vs Ink
manvsink.com

Manual
manualcreative.com

Margot Harrington
pitchdesignunion.com

Mark Pernice
maticart.com

Mash
mashdesign.com.au

Matadog Design
matadog.com

Matchstic
matchstic.com

Matt Chase
cargocollective.com

Matter Strategic Design
matter.to

Mélangerie Inc.
melangerienyc.com

The Metric System Design Studio
themetricsystem.no

Michéle Brummer-Everett
mlbeverett.com

Michelle Maguire
myohmyoh.com

Mikey Burton
mikeyburton.com

Mine
minesf.com

Mirko Ilić
mirkoilic.com

Mitchell Graphics Creative
mitchellgraphics.com

Modern 8
modern8.com

Mohamed Axlif
axlif.com

Moolee Bunnag
coroflot.com/mooleebunnag

Natoof
natoof.com

Nick Brue
nickbrue.com

Nikolaus Schmidt Design
nikolausschmidt.com

L'Office Optimiste
officeoptimiste.com

OMFGCo.
omfgco.com

Owen Gildersleeve
owengildersleeve.com

Peters
allanpeters.com

Plazm
plazm.com

Poff & Freimuth Unlimited
michaelfreimuth.com

Politanski Design
politanskidesign.com

Product Superior
productsuperior.com

Real Estate Arts
realestatearts.com

Re: Creative
recreative.com

RoAndCo Studio
roandcostudio.com

Root
thisisroot.co.uk

Salt + Pepper Press
thesaltpepper.com

S Design, Inc.
sdesigninc.com

Shine Advertising
shinenorth.com

Square Feet Design
squarefeetdesign.com

State Digital
statebuilt.com

steinzeit-mediandesign
steinzeit-mediendesign.de

Steve Scott Graphic Design
stevescottgraphicdesign.com

Stitch Design Co.
stitchdesignco.com

Tad Carpenter Creative
tadcarpenter.com

Tether
tetherinc.com

Think Packaging
thinkpack.co.nz

Thumbcrumble
thumbcrumble.com

studiotwentysix2
studiotwentysix2.com

Urban Influence
urbaninfluence.com

The War on Mars
thewaronmars.com

Watson and Company
watsonnyc.com

Weiden + Kennedy
wkstudio.bigcartel.com

Westervin
westervin.com

X-Sight
xsd.com.au

Zinnobergruen
zinnobergruen.de

Zync
zync.ca

ABOUT THE AUTHOR

Public School is an Austin-based creative collective composed of designers, illustrators, and photographers. Together they've created work for clients such as *GOOD*, LIVESTRONG, NIKE, *New York Times* magazine, Conde Nast, and Chronicle Books.

ACKNOWLEDGMENTS

Public School would like to thank everyone who contributed to this book, especially those that took time to contribute essays: Jett Butler, Loz Ives, Roanne Adams, Kelli Anderson, and Owen Gildersleeve. Your input was incredibly valuable in shaping this work. Thanks to Madeline Good for helping from start to finish, from the organization of submissions to the design. Last, thanks to everyone involved at Rockport for your advice, effort, and most important, patience in making this book. You are all troopers.